Are you getting _all_ your library offers you? ---

IN
Books
Magazines
Newspapers
Pamphlets
Government Documents
Pictures
Maps
Phonograph Records
Sheet Music
Story Hours
Information Service

PUBLIC
LIBRARY
SYSTEM
MILWAUKEE

THE BRETHREN

ANNE ARNOTT

Frontispiece

THE BRETHREN

An Autobiography of a Plymouth Brethren Childhood

BY

ANNE ARNOTT

LONDON

A. R. MOWBRAY & CO LTD

© *A. R. Mowbray & Co. Ltd., 1969*

Printed in Great Britain by
Alden & Mowbray Ltd
at the Alden Press, Oxford

SBN 264 65578 8

First published in 1969

To my Husband
who reconciled my worlds

They sought no reward, and
they held the world well lost . . .

CONTENTS

ACKNOWLEDGEMENTS

This book owes much to several people. I should like to express my gratitude to my husband and certain friends, who urged me to write it; to those who willingly typed and re-typed the manuscript in their spare time; and especially to Canon William Purcell without whose invaluable advice and encouragement it might never have been completed.

FOREWORD

By Canon William Purcell

IT is not often the good fortune of a reader of many manuscripts to find one come into his hands which he knows at once is a minor masterpiece. Yet that was my own experience when the manuscript which ultimately, after many revisions and much polishing, eventually made this book of Mrs. Arnott's, came into my hands. Here are many things felicitously combined; tender memories of a childhood in a Plymouth Brethren household, of which the head was Mrs. Arnott's father, a consultant physician; vivid memories of growing up and growing out of the confines, devout and high-principled as they were, of that particular environment; a swiftly-moving narrative of work and life in the years of the Second World War when Mrs. Arnott was a schoolmistress, and when she met the naval officer who ultimately became her husband. But I think the chief merit of the book, apart from the great interest of its subject, is its vivid and loving characterisation. There was obviously great love between father and daughter; and few who read this book will be unaffected by the vividness of her recollection of him and by the love for him which has survived the changes and chances of the years, and which persists still, long after his death. The same could be said of her memories of her mother. These two are among the main characters of a book which is rich in many. Not surprisingly, perhaps, since Mrs. Arnott took a degree in English and later taught that subject, the book is also extremely well written. Now, as wife—her husband, until recently a solicitor, has recently been ordained—mother of two sons and a daughter, occasional teacher and a practising magistrate in her own part of the country, Anne Arnott looks back on a slice of life which, among the many other things it can do to a reader, shows just how rich and at the same time how curious human life can be.

PROLOGUE

IT was a queer childhood. No-one outside its own particular frontiers could really penetrate the disciplines and emotions so urgently enforced and felt, and a peculiar barrier existed between the world outside, with all its pulsating and fascinating life, and the inner apparently ordered calm.

I was brought up among the Plymouth Brethren. Now that these words sometimes suggest something rather disgraceful, and certainly heretical, to the world at large, owing to the extraordinary excesses of an extreme and unfortunate splinter group, the publicity given to these quiet, often withdrawn people, has been out of all proportion to their significance. Even the National Press has tried, without real success, to penetrate into the life led by the members of this body, who refuse to be known as a sect.

Here then, are some pictures of the life of a child, who grew up in an atmosphere almost totally unknown nowadays, hidden from ordinary people who neither cared for it nor sympathised with it, scenes of a period gone for ever. To many people today these may seem unbelievable, the emotions quite unreal. But I have set them down just as they were for me then. Yet life was not all a straightjacket. It had its own laughter, and tears, and peace, of a sort. But always there was the deep desire to be part of a world denied and ignored.

This is a personal story, written with great hesitancy, about a conflict between loyalty and freedom. I was neither able nor willing to abandon my loyalties to a people who showed me nothing but kindness. Yet ultimately I had to leave them. I have, sometimes, like others before and since, been asked why. This book is an answer.

I

MY PARENTS

My mother was very ill in a Nursing Home, dying, I heard the maids say, in hushed whispers.

My father, an able consultant physician, devoted and affectionate, was obviously too harassed to tell me anything.

An elderly but lively Anglican maiden aunt had arrived to look after the house and me, and to keep me amused when I was not at school, and she organised a rousing game with the drawing room cushions, giving them each a character and a life of their own. They became a family of mischievous children, and thumping punishment had to be meted out. But behind this drama which I played with a sort of despair, a doom seemed to have settled on the house. My mother, a Vicar's daughter, had had a shining academic career; she had married my father in her mid-thirties after rising to the top of her teaching profession. My father was a widower with two teenage daughters, and he thereupon added me to his brood—an afterthought if ever there was one. My mother who was gay but dutiful, had submerged herself and her talents in my father's life. She was my world, and if she went there would be nothing left. I was six years old.

That night I lay wakeful and unhappy, and at last climbed out of bed, feeling my way in the darkness. I was conscious of the rough haircord nursery carpet underfoot, then came the polished cold of the passage, and I reached the top of the stairs where I sat forlorn, my face pressed against the bannisters, through which I gazed anxiously down to the floor below.

Light streamed out from the open door of the drawing-

1

room, and my father coming up from the ground floor stepped into its soft glow, and I saw that his face was tired and drawn. He entered the room and was lost to sight, but I heard him press the electric bell on the wall which gave two sharp rings.

Thus summoned, as they were every night, the maids then began their nightly pilgrimage from the basement kitchens of our tall Georgian house. This journey took a little time, and puffing and blowing, Alice, Gladys and Lucy, cook, parlour-maid, and housemaid, arrived to sit in a row in the drawing-room for family prayers.

Alice, plump and comfortable, had a kind simple heart. She wore her straight hair in a mouse-coloured bun. Gladys, very modern as it seemed then, used to have her hair frizzed with hot curling tongs. Her caps and aprons were always immaculately starched and white. Lucy, the housemaid, tall, gentle, and slightly melancholy with soft doe's eyes, was equally neat. Later, much to my disgust—because I was very fond of her—she married an undertaker.

As I sat there motionless, listening, I heard the sound of quiet words,

'We ask thee, if it be thy holy will, to lay thy hand this night on her who is sick. Restore her to us we pray, if it be thy holy will, for thy name's sake . . .'

My mother recovered.

The horror that had secretly engulfed me for three months, that she might not come back, never left me. She made the gaiety in my life. She had an irrepressible humour that always burst out in the most troublesome circumstances, a staunch common sense in the face of difficulty, and a fascinating ability to mimic the pompous and the pretentious, although I think she had perhaps stifled her desire for frivolity in a very busy and involved life of public service.

She was my link with 'the world' and all its beckoning

pleasures and desires, the world that miraculously seemed not to touch my father, although he worked in it to heal its sick with a selfless devotion and energy.

He was a man who walked unselfconsciously and humbly with his God. Sometimes I tried to stumble after him, but I was always left behind.

. . . . .

My parents both came of unusual and lively families.

My mother was the eldest of three children of a London Vicar, a brilliant sometimes unruly family, full of untiring vigour and initiative. Sometimes, lying on the rug in front of the drawing room fire, I saw them all through her eyes. One year, a group of gypsies, with a small travelling circus, who regularly camped on the nearby common, came to the vicarage door to ask if the Vicar would go and minister to one of them who was dying. My grandfather immediately consented, but said that if he came he would like to hold a service for them on the next Sunday in their encampment. They agreed. On his arrival the following Sunday, he found them all ready and waiting for him, and they made him an improvised pulpit on the steps of the lion's den, and from here he preached to them. From then on, he was their close friend, and each year small and touching gifts of flowers or eggs were brought by them to the Vicarage door with the request that 'Daniel', as they now called him, would come back to preach to them from the same pulpit. This he did each year until his sudden death.

My mother's brother George, daring and wild, went to St. Paul's School, where he was earmarked by the High Master for the top classical scholarship to Balliol College, Oxford. He could compose Greek and Latin verse with complete ease. It was not so he first reached fame, however. One year the Thames had frozen over so that people could skate on it. When the thaw started, the ice broke up into shifting floes, jostling up and down the river. My uncle shouted to a group of school friends that he would cross the river by leaping from one moving ice floe to another. This he did with skill and *joie-de-vivre*, observed by horrified crowds on either bank, and so earned himself a paragraph in *The Times* under the heading 'Vicar's son risks life crossing Thames'. He never went to Oxford for his father died suddenly and tragically when he was still at school, and the family were left very badly off. A place was procured for him in the Admiralty, and here he rose to a very high position, earning the highest honours for his work in the first World War, including the French Order of the Legion of Honour, and the Japanese Order of the Rising Sun; and on one occasion he enjoyed the small drama of an entire train being run especially for him to take him from the South to the North of France when he needed to return to England from Malta, where he was in charge of arming the Allied fleets at that time.

The three Vicarage children were resourceful in providing their own amusements in a way that many modern children seem unable to do. On one occasion, tiring of the stream of rather dull visitors to the Vicarage, they planned a small enterprise. A stout stick, strong twine and a bent pin made an excellent and efficient fishing rod. Hiding themselves under the window-sill of a tiny room over the porch, they awaited the arrival of an unpopular lady parishioner who wore imposing hats. At the crucial moment as she stood on the step they deftly caught their unusual 'fish', and neatly hooking the hat, they lifted it off the visitor's head, and into the room above. Dire wrath followed this escapade, and they were in profound disgrace.

My father also came of an original London family, 'a loving quarrelsome family', he described it. To his eternal annoyance he had seven sisters and no brothers. This large unwieldy family were all united in their devotion to their father and mother. A coloured miniature of my grandfather in his forties shows a noble face, lofty brow, and a calm and piercing gaze. His thick dark hair and luxuriant moustache and beard give him an imposing impression of controlled strength. Through a matter of conscience, and because of his view that 'the truth' as seen in the Bible was being stifled in many Churches, he left the Church of England, and joined the simple worship of some of the early Plymouth Brethren.

He ruled his family with love and discipline and after his faith, his chief passion was natural history. Every summer he arrayed his large family in thick brown home-made paper leggings, and led them on organised adder hunts on Exmoor.

Luckily for my father he was not deprived of male companionship. He had sixty-four first cousins in regular families of eight, many living within calling distance. The nearest cousins were a family of eight boys and one girl: all these families of cousins had in common great vitality and energy. Some of them reached the top of their professions. Harry Atkins became Governor General of New Zealand, and Richard Webster the Lord Chief Justice of England. My father's older sisters had intrepid hearts and untiring vigour. Edith and Lucy went out to China as missionaries in the days of the last great sailing ships, where Lucy died of typhoid fever. Annie became a nursing sister at St. Bartholomew's Hospital in the days before nursing was the established profession it is today.

My father went to a private school in Blackheath which he does not seem to have particularly enjoyed. In early years this was hardly surprising as the entire family was transported daily to their respective schools in a hansom cab, and as his school came first, his fate at school was sealed. The boy with seven sisters was a joke that caused him great morti-

B

fication. Later, he did his medical training at Guy's Hospital, coming top or top equal in his final examinations, and went on to become a dresser and houseman at Guy's; subsequently he was in charge of the Royal Waterloo Hospital for women and children. All his life he was devoted to children, and had a unique flair for dealing with them.

By the time I was born, he was a senior Consultant Physician in Bath, with one of the finest medical libraries in the city, a great knowledge of medicine, and a gift for diagnosis in difficult cases.

My mother, too, had made a satisfying career for herself. In some ways she was very modern for her times. She was among those who early took advantage of a full university education when it was first offered to women. She went to the Royal Holloway College at Egham in Surrey, later to be incorporated in the University of London. She cycled—in 'bloomers',—the first voluminous approach to trousers for women, and then thought rather outrageous. She played hockey in the college team, wearing a long skirt and blouse with stiff collar. Even worse, in Victorian eyes, she rode pillion on one of the earliest motor-cycles belonging to a friend. She was a convinced Suffragette, although not militant, and above all she found the academic life enthralling and satisfying. Yet she was a very feminine woman in the best sense of the word, and never advanced the cause of women's rights in an unnecessarily vociferous way. She generally won her point by gentle reasoning. She never, apparently, looked 'the blue-stocking'. I remember meeting a female college don who had taught with her at a famous Edinburgh School:

'Your mother always dressed so well', she said. 'I still remember her lovely blouses, pretty and immaculate. She always looked so fresh and pretty. I envied her tremendous ability.'

Her first teaching experience in a well known girls' public boarding school, the Royal School for Army Officers' daughters in Bath, would be regarded with horror nowadays. She had left London with first class honours in Mathematical Moderations, and every prize available including the Martin Holloway prize 'awarded annually to the best and most generally efficient student'. Her father had just died with tragic unexpectedness. The family of which she was the eldest, were left desperately poor, and she had only one pound to last the whole of her first term until her salary was paid. On arrival at the school, the stern and extremely Victorian headmistress gazed at her disapprovingly, her eye alighting on my mother's slightly jaunty and fashionable little hat.

'I am afraid you must go out and buy a bonnet immediately', said the Head. 'We cannot possibly have you in that hat here.' Utterly crestfallen, she was sent into the town to purchase for ten precious shillings a respectable Victorian ladies' black bonnet. She spent three years at this school, obviously earning the affection and respect of the staff, in view of what happened later.

She was now appointed Senior Mathematical Mistress at George Watson's Ladies' College, Edinburgh. Here, she said, in some ways she was happier than she was at any time in her life. The mood and intellectual quality and vigour of Edinburgh life appealed deeply to her, for there was a streak of earnestness and idealism in her make-up which fitted in with her circle here. These girls were keen and anxious to learn, and to make friends in off-duty times. Very often they took her out cycling to North Berwick, or climbing the local hills, and Arthur's Seat. Here she became a sincere admirer of that great Church of Scotland divine, Dr. Alexander Whyte. Visits to concerts, the theatre and lectures, added the riches of the arts. Her life was full, but not—

at first—easy. She had two specialists and ten more generally qualified staff directly under her, and most of them were older than she was. One elderly man on first seeing her had declared he would not serve under 'that young upstart'. My mother had been appointed on the grounds of exceptional academic attainment, and the famous Headmistress backed her up consistently. Eventually through my mother's work, the whole Mathematical Department was reorganised and put on a very sound academic basis.

During this time my mother studied in the evenings, and travelling down overnight to London, took as an external student, the B.A. degree in Mathematics and German, now available to women. In this she gained a double first.

She then became second mistress at Notting Hill High School, in London, which belonged to the Girls' Public Day School Trust. But while here, the bombshell fell. She was only twenty-nine, and she received a letter asking her to apply as Headmistress of the Royal School, Bath, where she had held her first post. She refused, not once, but twice. The third time her old college principal intervened, urging her most strongly to apply. Eventually, with a sinking heart she allowed an application to go forward, and was appointed.

The next five years were certainly a high test of her ability. It was a lonely position, she sometimes said in her reticent way, rather typically not revealing anything of the real depths of her feeling. One of her achievements that much pleased her, was rather an odd one. She bought some pigs to devour the refuse from the kitchens, and so ensured a good supply of bacon for the school at no cost. She planned the more intensive growing of food in the large kitchen gardens, and in many ways helped to put the school on a sound economic basis.

She led an interesting life in many ways, and met outstanding and unusual people. The great Lord Roberts of

Kandahar, of Boer War fame, Commander-in-Chief of the British Army, sent his niece to be educated under her. He was a little man, of great courtesy, with a dynamic character. Sometimes they used to walk in the extensive grounds together, while he talked of the small girl, who was his ward.

It seemed she was set for the highest academic career, and she said that she had put the thought of marriage from her. But during the illness of certain girls she would talk to the school medical officer, and so it was that she first met my father. I think she must have seen a kind, dedicated and lonely man, with a sense of humour breaking through now and then, who had in common with her a deep inner seriousness of spirit. He told me, in after years, how he used to watch her with the girls and noticed her sympathy and care for them and a certain shy charm.

'So I fell in love with your mother', he said simply.

He was fifteen years older than she was, had two teenage daughters, and devoted sisters who ran his house, and entirely differing views on religious practice. Their unlikely marriage, in face of doubts, difficulties and opposition, and perhaps misgivings on both sides, took place. My mother was as devoted to my father when he died as in those early days. He was her life, and I think, her refuge. In the end she lived only a year longer than he did, having retreated into some grievous distant place of her own when he died, saying 'Why couldn't I have gone too?'

It seemed we could not reach her or help her. Perhaps, in a way, she had already gone with him.

2

A QUIET HOUSE

I GREW up in a beautiful Georgian house in Bath built by
the famous Wood brothers. It was five stories high, not
counting the double basement and wine cellars beneath it.
Its eighteenth century neo-classical pillared front was
handsome and imposing. The large deep area surrounded by
iron railings was to the right of the front door, and down its
steep flight of stone steps the tradesmen descended to the
kitchen regions where 'the servants' lived, as they were called
at that time.

I was only allowed in the large old-fashioned kitchen on
special occasions, such as the evening when the stirring of the
Christmas puddings took place. Next door to this was
another large dark room, traditionally called the house-
keeper's sitting-room. In the dim light, the vast deep cupboards rising to the ceiling stored many fascinating objects of
family history, including a two foot square family Bible, and
many discarded Victorian objets d'art. On one side of the
room stood two outsize glass cases. In one of these a large
stuffed dog, faintly Airedale by breed, stood *en garde*, on a
little faded grassy mound, a dead pheasant at his feet. In the
other, surprisingly enough, was a staggeringly robust
albatross, with unwinking eye of lurid yellow. A tired-
looking fish appeared to have fallen at its feet.

In one corner of the room, still resplendent although
past his youth, the largest strongest dapple grey rocking
horse I have ever seen, forever galloped forward on his wood
and iron stand. Every Saturday morning I rode him over
distant plains and prairies while my mother sat at a round

table to 'do the laundry'. An enormous basket would be filled to the brim by the housemaid while my mother made the lengthy entries in a hard notebook. Later in the morning an aged man, with an equally aged grey pony and cart, arrived at the area gate. He would descend the steps slowly and enter the house, and soon would emerge again struggling with the large laundry basket which was being propelled at the rear by Alice and Gladys, heaving and struggling to get it up the steps, until at last it was put into the cart which clattered away over the cobbles.

The consulting rooms were on the ground floor, one bearing the word 'Inasmuch' in a frame over the door. I knew what it meant. Although this was not its intention, it was a constant reminder to me that all my father did was for the sake of his Master. 'Inasmuch as ye have done it unto the least of these my brethren, ye have done it unto me.' The object of the greatest interest to me here stood concealed in a dark cupboard in the small consulting room—it was the complete skeleton of a man. Often I wondered who it had once been. Its mortality bothered me.

The dining-room, on the ground floor, was large and lofty. It was chiefly noteworthy for the enormous glass cases lining one wall. An amazing collection of stuffed birds and mammals crammed the shelves to capacity. All had been stuffed by my paternal grandfather, although it was claimed that none had been shot unless they were dead or ill, or were some menace to life. So a very large fighting cock, which had repeatedly accounted for a number of lesser birds, had pride of place. In contrast, a kingfisher, wrens, a jay, sea gulls, a curlew, a delightful little puffin, a crow, some starlings and many other varieties of bird jostled together. From among their legs peered a weasel, a stoat, some field mice and harvest mice, and perched above them, a red squirrel gnawed at some nuts. Every spring, with a groan, my mother donned a lavender overall and put a sort of mob cap over her auburn hair; the maids then laid out special brushes, polish and dusters, and amid general depression at the size of the task, the birds received their annual spring cleaning and grooming. It was a wonderful sight to see them standing all around the room on their polished wooden stands filling the large floor space. I would stroke their soft sleek feathers, my finger tips tingling with the sensuous pleasure this gave me.

The dining-room also was the scene of another custom, long since lost. Every month I believe it was, an anxious-looking man in a buff overall arrived to wind the clocks of the house, and adjust them to Greenwich mean time.

Ascending the stairs again towards the drawing-room, the eye was arrested on the half-landing by two hideously healthy specimens of the aspidistra, much loathed by my mother. Pressure from her sisters-in-law made her feel compelled to keep them, much against her will. She tended them with care and exasperation.

On the first floor the drawing-room was my mother's sanctum; as I look back, it forms in my mind a mental picture of 'gracious living'. It was a beautiful lofty room with a white marble Adam fireplace and unusual Chinese blue hearth tiles. The blue green carpet was restful, but my joy lay in the two wonderful rugs,—full skins of a lioness and a leopard, their heads forming pleasant little bumpy seats, while they snarled forever into the distance. Not inappropriately, the leopard was partly shaded by an immense potted palm tree. These rugs had been sent by two missionaries to my father. Two large glass-fronted mahogany curio cabinets stood in two corners of the room, containing rare and wonderful curios and treasures, many from Africa and especially China, including a Ming vase.

Each afternoon the parlourmaid would bring up afternoon

tea to this room, carried on a large burnished copper tray. The silver tea-pot and hotwater jug would shine and twinkle in the firelight on winter afternoons. Here I lay on the lion skin reading for many hours, and in this anyway I had great freedom, choosing my own books in the public library, and spending birthday present money on books of my own. Gradually what I did not experience in the world, I taught myself at second hand, and lived through the lives of other people, often totally unconscious of my surroundings. Life was a wonderful adventure. I could hardly wait for the day when I would myself experience all its excitements and emotions.

Upstairs on the next two floors were six bedrooms, many odd cupboards in which you could hide yourself, and the bathroom. Outside one of the attic bedrooms was a large flat roof space called 'the leads', where one could sit and gaze out over the rooftops, and away to the hills. The flowering chestnut tree in the garden beneath had a history. The owner of the house in 1836 brought a chestnut home in his pocket from the Gardens of the Tuilleries at Versailles. This he planted at the end of our garden. It grew into the largest tree of its kind in the county, its blossoms of an unusually deep pink. As one sat up there, dreaming among the chimney pots on a summer evening, the sky turning rose-red in the west, the church bells of the Abbey could be heard leaping and echoing over the city, and as the sun disappeared over the distant rim of the hills, the branches of the trees grew dark against the sky.

The whole house had an atmosphere of quiet dignity and security. It sheltered you, embraced you, and hid you from the world outside, and its sounds spoke of permanence and peace. The clocks had different voices but one theme. The dining-room clock had a heavy soft tick, comforting, reassuring, a trifle drowsy; the brass clock in the front consulting-room had a busy brisk note; but the golden carriage clock in the drawing-room had a melodious sweet chime, telling of graciousness and comfort.

The sounds and smells of 'below stairs' penetrated only dimly, as if from far away. Remoter still, lay the basement and cellars, wrapped in deep silence, broken only, when one daringly entered their dark cavernous depths, by the tiny rustle of mice, or the soft tap of one's own shoes on the cold stone floors.

It was a house where adults lived an ordered sober life. To be a child there was to walk alone, stepping curiously through the quiet rooms which had seen nearly two hundred years of life.

3

THE MEETING

SHORTLY after my mother's illness, when I was six years old, I was given a large Bible for Christmas, my first grown up copy of the Authorised Version. This was chosen by my father with suitably large print so that my eyes should not be strained because of the daily necessity of reading a passage from it. I still remember the delicious smell of the leather covers, the luxury of the golden-red outer edges to the pages and the smell of the printed paper. My pleasure in it was sensuous, but let no one think I did not appreciate it. It was to be my book of rules, my charter to Heaven, the scroll of Christian journeying through Vanity Fair. In my father's firm clear handwriting there was an inscription on the flyleaf after my name and the date,

'Thy Word is a lamp unto my feet, and a light unto my path.' Psalm 119. 105.

I still have it, rebound in stiff covers now, the ink of the inscription fading, and its outer glories gone, but I feel its power, for was it not the message of God to me, small and insignificant, and always lagging behind, finding the faith difficult while the Saints soared on?

Clasping it firmly under my arm this Christmas morning, dressed in my new winter coat with the last word in luxury— a soft brown fur collar and fur cuffs over blue cloth—I trotted out to the Meeting with my parents.

Here was the very centre of life for 'the Saints', as the Brethren sometimes used to allude to each other. My father belonged to the Open Brethren. This meant he belonged to the largest and least exclusive group of 'p.b.'s' as many called them, for they would welcome any committed Christian from outside denominations to join their Communion Service or the Lord's Supper as it was called. This group was really quite orthodox, believing in the Anglican Creed, but not in infant baptism; however they had no Minister or Priest. For 'the Saints' ministered to each other as the Spirit led them, and to this extent there was some similarity to a Quaker Meeting, but their entire and ultimate authority was the Bible, which to them was the literal inspired word of God. The Meetings were carried out as nearly as possible like the first meetings of the early Christian Church, so far as this can be gathered from the writings of the Apostle Paul.

There was never financial difficulty, for the Brethren generally 'tithed' their income, tending to err on the side of giving more rather than less, and always gave of their income 'as they were led', so that there was always enough for the Meeting's modest needs. Small wooden money boxes were strategically situated at the two entrances, each suitably labelled: 'Hall Expenses'; 'Missions'; 'The Poor'. Every Sunday I had two pennies, and I was always deeply exercised as to which box should receive my all. In the end it was always 'The Poor'. I remember overhearing a motherly old lady remark in her soft west country accent, the broad 'r's' still nostalgic in my memory, 'Dear little soul, she don't never forget the Poor.' I swelled with a wholly unrighteous spiritual pride. Poverty was one thing I did not suffer, but neither did I live in a home where material possessions were thought valuable. Money was carefully and thriftily spent. Luxuries were rare.

That Christmas morning I took my seat as usual between my mother and father on the exceptionally hard pew seat. Close behind us sat two of my elderly aunts, attired in black. One, a spinster, with a large brimmed pudding-basin hat, was always affected by a loud cough during the meeting, which caused the hat to vibrate to and fro. A cough lozenge would be produced by my father looking as nearly irritated as one so patient and tolerant could look. The other aunt, a widow, fell as usual into a heavy doze, her mouth falling open, so that an occasional soft snore was heard. My mother would then lean back and gently prod her, at which she would sit up looking very indignant.

To my grief this day, the Christmas story was barely mentioned, for the Brethren did not believe in celebrating any special days or festivals. The Incarnation was to be born in mind at all times, but never one time. No flowers decked the large bare hall, whose only adornment was an immense text in gilt letters which read 'God is Love'. Ignoring the ministry of those leading Brethren who felt moved to centre their theme, as usual, on the Crucifixion, I surreptitiously turned the pages to finger out the Christmas story, and breathless, I was removed from the plain drabness of my surroundings. The eternal drama of the Birth at Bethlehem glowed like a fire before my eyes, the night sky, dark blue, pinpricked with stars, became brilliant as the throbbing silvery light of one star flooded down onto the roof of the Inn. Strange unearthly music echoed in the frosty heavens, and warmed and strangely excited in my heart, I, too, crept to the stable door to watch with the shepherds . . .

Was not this a day never to be forgotten? Why could we not hear about it, then, on this Christmas morning? Already I was full of many questionings which led me on a long journey before I ever came near to finding any satisfactory answers.

Unlike the dreadful Christmas Day experiences of Edmund Gosse in his recollections *Father and Son*—his father was one of the very strictest and most rigid of the early Plymouth Brethren—when a Christmas pudding was not even permitted in the room, because it was 'the food of idols', our Christmas Day was quite normal after the morning was over.

All spinster relatives, or widowed aunts and cousins, or lonely people, were invited to a traditional Christmas lunch. Crackers were pulled, paper hats worn, simple presents distributed. Sometimes my father dressed up as Father Christmas with great enjoyment and a wealth of drama; and fishing under the potted palm tree in the drawing room he would distribute the pile of presents to everyone.

During the evening it was rather moving when old patients from his medical mission—where he gave free skilled treatment to many poor folk each week—would arrive at the door with a flowering plant or bunch of flowers for 'Doctor', often with pathetic gratitude that he had saved this or that one's life. Year after year, a burly cheerful middle-aged man arrived with his rosy little wife and his little smiling daughter to bring my father a gift and show off his family. This was Charles, who had been my father's coachman, in the days of the carriage and pair, and then became his chauffeur, until the first World War. He would pump my father's hand up and down, often with tears of pleasure in his eyes at seeing 'Master' again. The year's history of events would be related, and my father's face would be alight with a kind and beaming smile. He was entirely unselfconscious.

During the evening my mother and father relaxed and looked at their Christmas cards, and their own presents together. My father was always naïvely incredulous at kindness shown him. However there was an exception. Wealthy patients had a habit of sending him expensive pieces of silver. The only uncharitable comment I ever heard him make concerned one of these. He examined an ornate silver bowl, an eighteenth century antique of some beauty. Turning it over in his hands, and reading the new and fulsome inscriptions to himself on it, he frowned.

'Dear me', he said, 'I do wish they would stop giving me their old silver, and would pay their bills.'

Sundays were to be regarded as holy days, a day of rest for those who worked, and a day of quiet for all, when the spirit of man could contemplate the things of God, and attendance at the morning meeting at eleven was obligatory. Through sun, rain, hail or thunder the mile and a half walk was undertaken, if necessary in oilskins and under a large umbrella, but never in a car. A few years before my father had had the carriage and pair driven by Charles the coach-man. Now that he drove his own small car, it was used entirely for the medical practice. Walking was of course more healthful and more economical! On arrival at the meeting, the dripping outer garments would be removed if the weather was bad, amid hearty handshakes and greetings, and solicitous whispered enquiries after one's health.

One day a worldly cousin accompanied us at her own request, out of kindness I thought, or affection for my mother. Now any stranger had to be introduced to the 'Saints'. If one was 'in' the Brethren, a letter of commendation extolling our dear brother or sister, or commending them to the care of the meeting was received from the elder Brethren in the area to which the visitor belonged. If one was a member of 'one of the sects', always considered unsound in some particular or other, then one must have other recommenda-tion. On this occasion my father murmured at length into the ear of the leading brother. What *would* they say, I wondered. Cousin Madeline was, deliciously, not 'one of us'. She wore a lot of coloured wooden beads, and powdered her nose a good deal, and even ventured on a little lipstick, not so widely used then except by the very fashionable. She painted beautiful miniatures, and was sprightly. I listened with bated breath. The usual list of visitors commended from one Brethren 'Assembly' and another was read out, and now:

'Also we have with us, Miss Dennis, known to be a believer.' Horrors! What would Cousin Madeline think of this? However, all was well.

'Dear Lou', she said with a giggle afterwards, gripping my mother's arm, 'do you know I was amazed to hear what they said about me. At first I thought that man said, "Also with us is Miss Dennis, known to have been in Geneva!"'

The Sunday meeting took the form of hymns, prayer and 'ministry'. The hymns were taken from a sober volume called *Hymns of Light and Love*; these were sung without organ or piano which might have proved a distraction to weaker spirits, and a large and benign elder brother would raise the tune in a piercing if unmusical tenor. Then we were off. The sound would rise and fall, faintly reminiscent of the un-accompanied singing in the simple services in the Gaelic I have heard in mission churches in Wester Ross. Somehow there was a pathos and a longing:

'The sands of time are sinking,
    The dawn of heaven breaks,
The summer morn I've sighed for—
    The fair sweet morn awakes.
Dark, dark hath been the midnight,
    But dayspring is at hand,
And glory, glory dwelleth in Immanuel's land.'

This hymn threw me into melancholy. I found the mornings on earth fair and sweet, and did not want to be translated to another sphere. But my father would look so distant and sad, and yet with a kind of holy joy as well, that I wondered if he was thinking of heaven—or perhaps his first wife to whom he had been deeply devoted, who died after eight years of a supremely happy married life. I was told by one of

my aunts that he had gone nearly mad with grief at that
time. I believe I may have been the only one who asked
questions and talked about that period of my father's life
to him. And oddly enough, it was to me he confided the
story of his first marriage. He had waited twelve years
before she had consented to marry him, but he said he had
never faltered in his love for this nursing Sister of Guy's
hospital. She had come of a county family used to a social
life, to riding her own horse and to hunting. She had given
up all this to dedicate herself to the care of the sick, and my
father wanted no other woman.

I must say I felt exasperated with her for keeping him
waiting for an answer to his regular proposals of marriage for
so long. But the Victorians never seemed to have discussed
their problems, and some misunderstanding lay between
them, chiefly because she was a devout Anglican and he
belonged to the Plymouth Brethren. His conscience would
not let him worship in any other way even if it meant death
to his deepest desires. Her photo, hanging in his room until
the day of his death—he seemed unable to see anything
incongruous in this—showed a tall grave woman with a direct
and fearless expression, yet not hard. She died, after eight
years of marriage, of the then incurable diabetes. His two
tiny girls, hardly more than babies, were delicate and pined
for her. He told me how he feared the elder would die of
grief, for she seemed to fade away after her mother's death.

So it was that this hymn I thought, seemed to stir some
deep memory in him. Generally the hymns in the morning
meeting would be entirely devotional, centring upon the
theme of the Crucifixion. There is no doubt that a very true
devotion to their Lord was in the hearts of those who gathered
around 'the Lord's Table', Sunday by Sunday. It was,
however, a devotion that was not, in one way, carried far
into the outside world. For the Brethren were to be 'separate'

C

from the world, so that their faith could be held more purely, and they could keep close to God with no hindrance or distraction. In some ways this might mean an almost 'monastic' seclusion of themselves and their families from close contact with 'unbelievers'.

The prayers were all extempore, sometimes at great length. I would sigh and shift up and down on the hard seat, and my idle gaze between the fingers half covering my eyes, would wander over 'the sisters' around me. Had they ever had passionate yearnings for gaiety, like me, I wondered? They seemed so peaceful and devout that I doubted it. I was sure they did not feel moved to abandon themselves to music and dance when they got home from the Meeting—like me. Their faces were shuttered, intent. What was wrong with me I wondered, that my spirit stayed so persistently on the ground, while they all seemed to be translated, temporally anyway, into the heavenly realms?

The 'Ministry' consisted of the reading of the Word— of exposition variable in content. Sometimes I heard it beautifully and devoutly expressed, and sometimes it was instructive in the hands of a cultured or academic 'brother'— and there were a few of these. On the very rare occasions that he was moved to speak, my father showed complete sincerity, and his love for his Master shone out of all he said. But in the hands of the inept, it could become excessively tedious. 'Not, I felt, to profit', my father would say briefly, and that was the only criticism he ever made.

The whole of the morning service, however, centred on the 'Lord's Supper', and the great simplicity of their manner of receiving this Sacrament held something of real value. The table on which the elements were placed stood among the people. After prayer, the large loaf of bread was broken and divided onto four pewter plates, and these were then passed from one to another, each taking a morsel. The wine was poured into four large goblets and these were also passed from one to another. That there was real devotion and pure worship at this time I am sure. Often as he knelt in prayer and meditation, remote from the world and all around him, I have seen tears in my father's eyes. He had suffered greatly from the hostility of some members of his family to this, his way of worship, but he truly felt it to be the right way, most nearly like that prescribed for the early churches in the New Testament.

His position in the meeting was odd. Greatly loved by many whose doctor he was, admired for his deep integrity and sincerity of character, attractive by reason of the errant humour that burst out of him from time to time, he was nevertheless in one respect unacceptable. Both his first and second wife had been members of the Church of England. Worse, his two elder daughters had now become ardent Anglicans, and were frank and outspoken and even hostile in their criticisms of the Plymouth Brethren. To the meeting elders this was a sign, that loved as he was, he had been willing to marry those with 'unsound' views, particularly in the matter of infant baptism and confirmation which they held to be profoundly 'unscriptural'. The reference to the 'regeneration' of infants in the Anglican baptismal service was intolerable to them. They held that this sacrament might only be given rightly to young 'believers' or committed Christians. Similarly they held that confirmation was wrong, because they believed that it was in accepting Christ as a personal Saviour that a man received the gift of the Holy Spirit. There is no doubt that these are deep and difficult controversies. But the Brethren were unable to concede that other views might be an aspect of the same truth, seen from a different point of view. Moreover, because of his elder daughters' attitude, they held that my father had failed to bring up his family in 'the Truth'.

For these reasons he was never made an elder—although
he was, I believe, 'greater' in the faith than almost any man
there, for he followed his Master in deep humility, and of all
men loved lost humanity for whom Christ died.

I doubt if anyone nowadays could remotely imagine or
believe the climate of thought in which I lived. The
Plymouth Brethren lived in a sincere and daily expectation
of our Lord's Second Coming to earth. So it was that about
this time the Meeting held an ever increasing dread for me.
The chief of the elders, an erudite learned Greek scholar,
with a vast knowledge of Biblical exegesis, a loving impetuous man, inclined to pour out his feelings in words, felt
that the perils of 'the last days' must ever be laid before us.
It was his mission, drawing conclusions from Bible prophecy
and world events, and Scriptural allusions to the Jews
return to Palestine, to remind us constantly of the possible
imminent appearing of our Lord. This thought was beautiful
to my father. Was there any other hope more wonderful
than this—to see the Christ he loved and served?

But to me it was a thought of terror. How could I be *sure* I
was one of those who belonged to the Lord and who would
be 'caught up' to meet him on his return? For in all their
terrible majestic sonority the words of Paul in the epistle
to the Thessalonians were thundered forth, Sunday by
Sunday:

'For the Lord himself shall descend from heaven with a
shout, with the voice of the archangel, and with the trump of
God: and the dead in Christ shall rise first: then we which are
alive and remain shall be caught up together with them in
the clouds, to meet the Lord in the air: and so shall we ever
be with the Lord.' My eyes were full of the sight as legions of
angels in dazzling white purity filled the night sky, and the
piercing unutterable music of that heavenly trump cracked
through the very sense of hearing, and tore one; and down out

of limitless eternities of space soared the heavenly creatures,
stern, majestic, full of an intense vitality, filling the night
sky, blotting out darkness in searing light,—and One was in
the midst of them, and I could never look up. I knew my
heart was sinful, I would never be worthy to join that heavenly
throng, for I was as the smallest and poorest in the Father's
Kingdom, and my heart wept as I saw that I must be left
behind. 'Oh, Christ, don't leave me behind', I prayed between clenched teeth each night. There was no doubt that my
mother and father would be taken, and they would meet the
Lord in the air, but I would not be there. In these materialis-
tic days it seems impossible to believe in the awful reality of
my fears. But they were a torment and agony to me as a
child.

The horrifying picture drove me like Christian in the
beginning of *The Pilgrim's Progress* to a sort of despair. I
thrust the thought of the Second Coming to the back of my
mind; perhaps it would not come so soon—I tried vainly to
forget it. I could never speak of my dread to my parents.
Many times I tried, but the words stuck in my throat, my
mouth turned dry and stiff. My mother, I am sure, realised
something of my thoughts:

'Don't forget that a thousand years with the Lord are but
as a day', she would say. 'I think it is a mistake to try and
prophecy these things. Christ always said no one would know
the time of his coming.' A sort of wild hope would then
seize me, and I would hurl myself into my life at school, playing and working with an almost feverish intensity, for life was
precious, and every minute must be lived to the full. What
adventure, what dramatic encounter might not occur? I
savoured every joy, every friendship, every simple event with
a deep aware pleasure, because at the back of my mind I
knew that life was temporal.

On Sunday mornings the dread came back. I sat in the

Meeting now with fingers stuffed in my ears, for I could not listen any more. It was too disturbing. Sometimes I saw my mother looking sideways at me with troubled kindly gaze. But I would not listen.

And then it happened. It was night time I dreaded the most. Surely the Lord would come at midnight, for was it not then that the unwise virgins were sleeping, having neglected to get the necessary oil for their lamps, and who better than I could hear the wail of lamentation, 'Behold the Bridegroom cometh . . . ' It was a sultry sort of evening, the sky heavy and lowering with a strange greenish light. The trees in the nearby park swayed blackly across the sky and an uneasy wind stirred through them. My bedroom on the third floor had its window wide open, and as I lay in bed gazing out past the half drawn blind, I felt vaguely unhappy, and tossed and turned until I fell into an uneasy dream-ridden sleep.

I awoke with a terrible start, the room was shaking, and a sound that cut to my very heart echoed and thundered—it was the last Trump. No thunder storm ever sounded like this, with a terrible subterranean roaring and trembling.

I leapt out of bed, my one thought being to seize my mother before she was 'taken up'. I was sure I was too late. I screamed, but the sound was only a tiny choked cry, and I rushed like a tornado through the double doors and fell, more dead than alive, onto my mother's bed.

My terror was not so ill-founded after all. A real earthquake was felt all over the area at this time on that night, accompanied by strange sounds and tremors.

It was only some years later when, after hearing another prophecy of the Second Coming, even to the very date, June 4th, that a close school friend—clever and humorous, brought up in the Plymouth Brethren also—and I, were able to joke rather wryly. The weather was becoming hot and very sultry that summer. My friend leaned over from her desk, seized my wrist and muttered, 'Getting thundery towards June 4th.' Together we were overcome with silent shaking mirth at our own private joke that no one else could understand.

4

BE YE SEPARATE

Each year as the mild damp winter gave way to early Spring, and the first snowdrops broke through the wet lawns of the park nearby, I felt deep within me a breathless expectation that something significant was about to happen. Even now, I remember the choking sensation of excitement that often gripped me as I lay wakeful, waiting for the day to begin.

This particular day, which lingers in the memory, would have been the same, but for the insistent sound of heavy rain pattering endlessly on the window. The panes trembled with the drumming rhythm, and outside the water splashed and gurgled from the roof spouts.

Inside, in my dark retreat under the bedclothes, it was warm and secure, a shelter from the storm outside. Carefully I stretched out my fingers then clenched them slowly, as if hiding jealously the little moment of secret pleasure before morning came to break the enchantment. Often it was a relief to escape into a secret life of fantasy and imagination, because in real life I was made to feel apart from ordinary people, compelled to live as if an invisible wall surrounded me. How often and how curiously I gazed at the world outside, longing for its gaiety. How sadly I accepted the belief, which was constantly put before me, that the Lord's people were to be 'separate'. 'Come out from among them and be ye separate, saith the Lord.' This was the Biblical authority. There was no prevaricating. I was too young to understand the full implication, and it was clear that this was a fundamental priority with my father because of his desire to serve his Master with pure heart and dedicated intention. I could not question his sincerity. Now when I heard the lashing of the rain outside I could feel momentarily lulled in my security, warm in the enfolding love of my home. It was only when I came face to face with reality that I felt I was gazing through prison bars.

So now I peopled the darkness of my bed with a gay world of dancing fantasies, illumined with arrows of sunlight, while echoes of whirling music throbbed in my head. I stretched luxuriously, rolled onto my stomach, and there in the quiet before day broke, head resting on arm, I abandoned myself to pleasure.

A quick tap on the door and it opened. The world of fantasy fell apart. I uncovered eyes only, gazing out from a tiny opening in the bedclothes, to watch the tall slender figure of Lucy bend over me and put a cup of tea on a little table beside my bed. Beside it she put a tiny plate with a wafer of bread and butter on it, delicately thin. The plate was of white bone china, patterned with violets. It reminded me of the Spring woods, damp and sweet-smelling, with tiny clusters of dog violets half hidden in the undergrowth.

I watched Lucy as she went across the room to the windows, and saw her dress revealed in the grey rain-washed light as she drew up the first blind.

'The blue one's nicest,' I said ruminatively. She was wearing the grey and white striped dress which I thought was dull and dutiful. Lucy ignored my comment, and sharply pulled up the second blind, whose cord, with its wooden acorn swinging, clicked sharply against the pane. It was day.

The tea was China, and tasted smoky. I licked the butter off the bread, and crumpled the whole morsel into a ball in my mouth. It tasted more substantial that way. Distastefully, I gazed out of the window. Looking at the steady downpour, I knew I was doomed for mackintosh and umbrella. A nightmare! No one else at school was made to carry an umbrella.

It assumed hideous proportions in my mind, dwarfing the day with ignominy. Added to other trials, I would be an object of scorn, muffled and wrapped up as if I could not face the elements.

While I gloomily considered how I could avoid the situation, the door started to open again. I watched the thin brass drop-handle rise and turn, moved by an invisible hand outside. Instinctively, I knew my father was there. He stood, tall, grave and enquiring by my bed, his hair incongruously fluffy after his bath. He had arisen at six-thirty, as he did every morning, for private prayer and the study of the New Testament in Greek, and the Old Testament in Hebrew. He was self-taught, an achievement made possible by his deep passionate desire to read the Scriptures as closely as possible to the original.

'But why do you do it, why, Daddy?' I used to say to him.

'Darling, the riches to be found in the Bible are limitless. You have no idea what a thrill it is to discover fresh light on God's word.'

I was usually unconvinced, but this morning it was he who questioned me.

'Have you done your reading this morning?'

Evasively, I shook my head. 'Reading' meant only one thing. My father longed for me to do as he did, and read a daily passage in the Bible. Indeed his own rock-like strength of will and purpose were founded on this habit. He sat on the bed and looked compellingly at me. I could not avoid that steady gaze.

'Why do we give babies milk?' he said in a matter-of-fact voice. I knew all the answers, and generally it was easier to give the right ones than to stop and argue. 'To feed them properly.'

'Well, of course. If they did not get their daily milk they would starve and die. So it is with our souls you know. We are weak in the faith like tiny babies and need our daily spiritual food. We must have it or we shall surely die before we learn to listen and hear when our Lord calls us.' His voice became solemn, imperative, as he added, in his special tone for quoting the Scriptural words: 'As newborn babes, desire the sincere milk of the Word.' He sighed, lost in his own thoughts, and went towards the door, then turning back, found a passage in the New Testament and placed it in my hands. Just as he was leaving the room he remembered why he had come.

'Only ten minutes to bath time,' he said briskly, the sermon over.

My reading, however, was perfunctory. The day now beckoned, the dream world was gone. Life and energy suddenly flowed into me, and I jumped out of bed, thrusting my feet into warm woolly slippers, and putting on a soft blue dressing-gown. I ran to the window, pressed my nose against the cold pane, and gazed out. Away before me, the branches of the majestic plane trees glistened black and wet, swaying in the wind. Undeterred by the rain, the rooks flew to and fro, calling with harsh unceasing cries.

I looked down onto the broad cobbled road beneath, and the rivulets of water running in the gutters, and saw the short squint-eyed milkman, shrouded in an oilskin cloak, walking along, with heavy wooden yoke across his shoulders, off which were suspended two large cans of milk. He made his progress from house to house, going to the gate at the top of each area steps, where the cooks were waiting for him, holding out big white jugs. Or else he vanished down each area steps to entertain those who lived 'below stairs' with the morning's gossip as he poured the frothy milk into their jugs with his big measure.

Meanwhile, next door to my nursery, I was aware of a regular light thumping sound in my father's dressing-room.

Each morning when his devotions were over, a great brisk-
ness fell upon him. He would take off his warm dressing-
gown and seize his 'dumb bells' and do his exercises. These
wooden objects, about ten inches long, were shaped like a
woman's torso with generous vital statistics. Waving them
about, he would prance up and down, touching his toes, then
banging them above his head and behind his back. Then up
would go the left arm, then the right, and with a final whirling movement like a windmill in a gale he came to the climax
of the operation and stopped. Thus nourished by the Word,
bursting with physical and mental vitality he would start his
day. One sensed that he gazed out on life in serenity and
hope, and because his uncompromising and puritan way of
life was softened by a sweetness of character, it was difficult
ever to oppose him.

All the household had by now received a little tray with a
pot of China tea, and the thin parchment bread and butter.
'Not exactly a luxury, I feel,' my father once announced, for
he was opposed to any softness, 'I find the warm liquid is
invaluable in moving the bowels.' Necessity thus appeased
conscience and all were satisfied.

A shout from my father penetrated the wall. 'Bath time.
Hurry upstairs quickly.' He emerged from his room to hustle
me up the flight of winding attic stairs to the only bathroom
in the large house, where he flung a good-sized lump of rock
salt into the rather meagre tepid water. When he had departed, I stepped in and sat in this rather prickly sticky
mixture. This salt was regarded as a panacea for many ills. It
prevented sweating and chills, toned up the system, and
strengthened those who were prone to colds. As usual the gas
geyser was hissing in an alarming and explosive manner. It
was an extremely large copper structure and my distrust of it
was not unnatural.

One evening a violent explosion shook the house, while my

step-sister was in the bath. The three maids, my parents, and I rushed towards the attics, while clouds of thick steam poured down the stairs. Emerging, as out of fog, a damp pink kimono pulled a little inadequately around her, my sister emerged shaken but unharmed although, not surprisingly, indignant.

'The bally thing has blown up,' she announced, her voice rising to a wail, as the water trickled off her in a pool on the stairs.

'Nonsense,' said my father running past her up the stairs. His faith in the geyser's efficiency had always been unreasonable, I felt. But she was right. The ceiling was blackened, the top of the cylinder shattered. I always, therefore, regarded it suspiciously while I was in the bath.

All members of the household, not bathing, were taken large tin cans of water to their bedrooms by the housemaid. These stood on special mats beside the marble washstands with their flowered basins, ewers, and soap dishes. Visitors in the spacious high-ceilinged spare-room had a more complicated ritual. A large fluffy bath mat was placed in front of the gas fire. Then a generously-proportioned brown hip-bath was removed from its hiding-place in a curtained alcove, and placed on the mat together with very large cans of hot and cold water, carried up four flights of stairs from the kitchen below, and all was ready for the guest to climb out of the largest brass-knobbed double-bed I have ever seen.

On this morning, I dressed as usual and was ready by the time the electric bell in the hall rang twice and summoned the family to descend some eighty stairs to the dining-room. The breakfast was ready on the dining-table, concealed in various heated containers, which gave off tempting smells. But first things first. The three maids entered in an orderly row, murmured 'Good morning, Sir', to my father, smiled and nodded to my mother, and sat on three hard upright chairs in front of the ornate carved sideboard. My mother and the family took their places on the softer chairs, and my father, now immaculate in a dark blue suit, took his seat at the head of the table whereon lay a Bible and the Book of Common Prayer. Gazing around, to assure himself that everyone was listening, he opened the Bible, smoothed the page, and began to read a Psalm.

'This poor man cried, and the Lord heard him, and delivered him out of all his troubles.'

I stored away the words for future use, but just now I did not need them, I thought. Yet, young as I was, I knew how deeply they affected him.

'I have been that "poor man" so often, darling,' he once said, his arm around my shoulder, 'and the Lord has never failed me.' At such moments it was warm and safe and comforting to be beside him. We did not, I sensed it so often, belong to the world outside, and here I was temporarily consoled by his deep caring love.

After the reading we all knelt, and my father read two prayers from the Anglican prayer book, chiefly for my mother's benefit, I believe, for most Plymouth Brethren prayed at length and extempore. With the all-pervading influence of my father's strong unshakeable faith, I was growing up grounded in the teaching that each day's work must be committed to the Lord, and that because of this, shoddy work was unthinkable, and dishonouring to him, for only one's best was good enough. This of course was good and wholesome, but could, at times, be exacting. Physical exhaustion, depression, unhappiness were never allowed as an excuse for deviation from this rule, which was absolute.

If, however, one was really in trouble, then no one could have had more sympathy.

'Darling, would you like to kneel down with me and tell the Lord about this?' my father would say. One knelt, clasping and unclasping one's hands in embarrassment, while he prayed with great simplicity as if his Master was beside him. Somehow the sorrow or difficulty would ease.

'Burdens are lifted,
Blind eyes made to see,
There's a wonder-working power
In the blood of Calvary.'

And so it was, for him. He would rise with a deep and penetrating smile, as if his spirit was renewed. Yet, in his time, he had seen sorrow enough.

Prayers over, the day rushed upon us. I choked down my breakfast, hoping to slip out of the house before my father noticed the rain. He had a fixed horror of rheumatism caused by wearing damp clothes, as one of his sisters had been bed-ridden for some years for this reason, it was thought. I must be protected from a like fate. I got a few steps down the path in the rain. Nemesis. He came after me, holding out the hated umbrella.

'You must take this.' His voice indicated that he was not prepared to argue. I took it, loathing it, and decided to walk to school by the round-about way, avoiding the main road, and passing through a long winding uphill lane, little frequented. It was known as The Shrubbery, because of its gloomy overhanging hedges, and dark stories were hinted at of evil men who might be lurking there, waiting to do us girls some unspecified 'mischief'. I must risk this fate for the sake of the umbrella. As soon as I was hidden and sheltered, and found that no one was about, I closed the now dripping object, and carefully slid it up inside my mackintosh, and pulled the belt tighter. So far, so good.

I reached school, and with some bravado, now pleasantly wet as every one else, I pushed open the green swing doors. Here one was immediately conscious of a pervading smell, not unpleasant, compounded of rubber shoes, damp coats, polish and disinfectant. My next task was harder. I eyed those around me very warily. It needed considerable expertise to remove the mackintosh in one deft movement, keeping the umbrella hidden inside it—so that no one should see it and mock—and to arrange it carefully on the peg, with the horrible object still shrouded within it. When this was achieved I breathed again, and leaving the cloakroom ran up the broad stone staircase, jumping two and three stairs at a time, and so reached the classroom.

At school I lived another life, carefree, often high-spirited, not over-conscientious, unless it was in the writing of English essays, when the mind could delightfully wander and explore. Sometimes, I suppose, I must have been something of a trial to the staff. On this morning, I remember, I suddenly felt urgently that the boredom of a French lesson had gone on long enough. It was necessary to stage a simple diversion. I suggested, in a whisper, to a friend sitting in the next desk— she later became a Headmistress to Royalty—that we would, apparently accidentally, collide in the aisle between desks, after presenting our books to Mademoiselle for correction, and that we would then fall to the ground as loudly as possible. This part of the plan we fulfilled with great success, and a shattering crash, and we lay prostrate and helpless with laughter, gazing at the ceiling. What we had not anticipated was that owing to the closeness of the desks we would become totally wedged, and unable to rise again.

The lesson became a riot, while Mademoiselle, in a frenzy of rage, waved her pince-nez over us, gesticulating madly, and gazing upwards, invoked the Deity to help her to control herself in dealing with such impossible girls.

Meanwhile at home the day proceeded as usual for my parents. Their life was full and busy. My father visited the hospitals where he was a senior Consultant, called on patients in their homes, and conferred with his colleagues over any

difficult case. Each afternoon he saw patients in his consulting-rooms at home. Normally there were often missionaries from all parts of the world as well as wealthy and
fee-paying patients. I remember meeting a number of them
from time to time who were invited to take tea in the drawing-
room upstairs after the consultation, and so I was fortunate
in meeting some remarkable characters.

I remember the Anglican Bishop in Jerusalem, kind and
humorous, an Anglican Bishop from China prone to gentle
teasing, and I can still see a formidable old lady missionary
from China. She was close on eighty, but full of vigour, and
refused to believe a Harley Street physician who had told her
she was virtually dying of heart disease. She told my father
that the Lord had told her that her work in China was not
yet finished. What did he propose to do about it? As always,
he began his examination with an open mind. He eventually
told her that in his judgement she was not diseased but he
believed her to have a large tumour pressing on the heart. He
said that an operation would be very dangerous at her age,
but might conceivably cure her. She never faltered. After a
very skilful surgeon had performed a brilliant operation, she
made a complete recovery, and incredibly went back to work
among her beloved women and girls until she was over
ninety.

Indelibly imprinted in my memory is the recollection of
the three wonderful missionary explorers, pioneers and brilliant writers, Mildred Cable, and Eva and Fransesca
French, who won fame after years as missionaries in China,
for their epic journeys across the great Gobi desert, northwest
of China, where no white man had ever been. Their journeys
were made so that they might take the gospel where it had
never been heard before, but in so doing, their achievements
became known and honoured across the world. They came to
visit my parents on various occasions over the years when on

D

furlough and small as I was, I knew as I gazed at them at tea, that here were people so unique and courageous that one's spirit was somehow lifted just to be with them. Miss Cable—the leader of 'The Three' in some ways—was small, sturdy and dynamic, with piercing blue eyes, and silvery white hair. On one particular day, she suddenly and unexpectedly turned to me, and gripped my hand, and smiled. Her whole face lit up and the relentless strength of expression was momentarily softened.

'Anne,' she said, 'I wonder if God will call you to China. Would you be ready to go?' I gazed back at her fascinated, feeling that if this small heroic woman summoned anyone to follow her, it would be impossible to disobey. Perhaps, and the thought came almost unwanted, if God ever called me, wayward and insignificant, I might feel that I must go or life would never be worth living again. I thought for a long significant moment, and the silence thudded in my head, and my throat was dry. Somehow, my answer was deeply important.

'Perhaps I would, if I knew I had to', I said. In that moment came the blinding realisation that all the pleasures of the world seemed tawdry and worthless and sad compared with the light in her face, and I recognised it for what it was. Had she called me, I would, I believe, have gone with her then. This encounter I have never forgotten.

My father loved his medical work for missionaries above all else. Turned down for 'the foreign field' as it was called, on health grounds when a young man, he thereupon vowed he would give his expert medical knowledge free to any missionaries who needed it, to enable them to continue in their work. I remember on many occasions being told by different people how he had, almost miraculously it might seem, saved their life when it was despaired of. In this work he earned the love and gratitude of many brave people. Our house was full of rare curios, ivory figures, beautiful skin rugs of animals, delicate china, all tokens of affection and gratitude from those from whom he would take no money.

My mother would be involved in her work too, I knew. Each day for her began with a solemn pilgrimage downstairs to the large basement kitchen to plan the day's menus with Alice, the cook, who was often to be found in a 'mood'. It speaks much for my mother's tact and patience that the house ran smoothly and Alice stayed with us for nearly twenty years. My mother herself never cared much for domesticity and fulfilled herself in various ways.

She had been a 'born teacher', which meant that she always kept something of the unsophisticated and eager spirit of a child, and imperatively, possessed a sense of the ridiculous which saved her from becoming autocratic. She was sympathetic, kind and academically outstanding, and she loved her 'girls', from teaching days, many of whom continued to visit her up to the time of her death. She found an outlet for her talents by working indefatigably for the educational life of our city, and became a Governor of many city schools, and a co-opted member of the City Education Committee. She was the first woman in the city who was asked to become a Justice of the Peace, but this honour she refused, feeling it would take up too much of her time.

Sometimes she buried herself in one of her chief academic hobbies, the study of Palestinian archaeology, about which she wrote learned articles which were published in some foreign journal. When life was frustrating she buried herself in a good detective story, or even a romantic novel, or busied herself with beautiful colourful embroidery.

If she found life in a Plymouth Brethren household rigid or limiting she never complained, for she was devoted to my father, who dominated her life. For this reason I believe that she stifled much of her own character and desires, and in later years grew reserved and withdrawn, refusing to discuss difficulties with family or friends. This loyalty took its toll. The expression of intelligence, kindness and merriment too often changed to one of strain and grief. She had a deep and sincere faith herself, but I think that in her own estimation she felt that she hardly measured up to my father's standards.

She had been a loyal member of the Church of England when she married my father, and I believe may have remained so at heart. But the difficulties were acute. When I was born she wanted me to be christened. This was difficult as the Brethren rigidly opposed infant baptism. It appears that a compromise was made, obviously with some difficulty, A personal friend, a certain Canon, came privately to the house, and I was ceremoniously baptised in the drawing-room with water from an ornate soap-dish. This somewhat odd situation, coupled with the realisation that other Plymouth Brethren were sharply criticising my father for not bringing her regularly to the meeting, and instructing her in 'sound' views which must be held if one was to be a true child of God, brought her to the eventual decision that she would join the Brethren. This she did, and thereby shocked her family. She grew more at peace in this milieu as time went on I believe, and she made a few close friends among the more broadminded of them, who really became very fond of her, relying on her judgement in many ways. But I grew to feel that she had sacrificed, willingly, her own identity, and I think it was done at great cost, how much we never knew.

So it was that the home I lived in was quiet, withdrawn from the outside world in many ways, and I, longing for amusement, would concoct some little drama from time to time, to enliven the days. On this particular afternoon, after the satisfying disturbance in the French class, I walked home slowly, content, and, as usual, was drawn back into another existence as I came to the tall Georgian house, and entered another world, where each day the realisation came afresh that my life was different, and in a way confined.

I rang twice on the door bell, banged impatiently on the fluted brass door-knocker, and when Gladys the parlour-maid opened the door, stepped into the quiet safe retreat.

'Where's mother?' My question was always the same, and there was always an undertone of anxiety. I had the perpetual fear that perhaps one day she would not be there. She was my link with freedom and the world. With her I became a person in my own right, not just a character to be moulded into an acceptable pattern, so guided, directed and watched over, that to withdraw into a secret life was the only freedom.

'Up in the drawing-room, and tea is ready,' Gladys answered, a little disgruntled at my impatience with the knocker. Relief swept through me. Home was safe and enfolding, and as yet I could not envisage life without it.

5

A BIRTHDAY AND A FUNERAL

SOMETIMES in a quiet secluded childhood like mine, certain days, or small happenings lived in the mind like a sunlit picture, assuming significance and meaning in the memory.

It was a fresh cool misty morning in the early Autumn, with the hint of sunshine to come. It would be hot later in the day with the heavy closeness that often wrapped our city. Now there hung in the air the crisp scent of wood fires. It was a happy morning and it was my birthday.

The family was not yet astir except for my father in his dressing room, lost in the study of the Greek New Testament. Downstairs, however, the maids were moving softly around and there was a sound of the clattering of cups and saucers as early morning tea was prepared.

My mother had secretly made me a magnificent Red Indian costume—for I was a tomboy. It lay in brown paper on the end of my bed and eagerly I unwrapped it, enchanted with the feather head dress and, above all, the trousers. Putting it on, I pranced up and down in front of the long mirror in my room.

It was time to be out and about, looking for adventure. Seizing my bow and arrow, I crept down the stairs and through the long hall into my father's smaller consulting room at the back of the house. I opened the double doors which led out onto a massive flight of steep stone steps descending to the garden beneath.

The morning air was cool and sweet and the grass of the lawn shimmered with the heavy dew. I gazed out over Red Indian territory. A camp fire must be lit quickly and I must procure food to cook on it.

I ran indoors again and turned to go down the steep dark stairs from the hall to the kitchen regions—stairs which were perpetually lit by electric light, as no daylight reached them. Now one entered another world. I entered the big kitchen, dark and interesting, whose heavily barred windows faced the front area, whose steps led up to the street, where it was fenced about with iron railings.

Alice, our cook, was sitting at a large wooden table in the centre of the room, elbows firmly placed on the white American cloth; a steaming white cup was clasped in her hands, from which she sipped noisily. Behind her the great black range with its massive ovens stretched along a good part of one wall. A fire was blazing behind its black bars and the flickering light of the cheerful flames was mirrored in the dark polished metal.

'*Please*, Alice, *please* may I have some paper and matches and wood and some potatoes?'

'Dear heavens, Miss Anne, what will you want next?' She rose, rather unwillingly. This room was her domain, forbidden territory to me, but she was good-natured at heart.

I waited impatiently. An enormous ginger and white Persian cat, which had been curled up, drowsing, in rather a shabby basket chair, rose, arched its back and deliberately spat at me. It had been a stray kitten, found by my father abandoned on the road with a severe head injury. He had nursed it, bathing and disinfecting the wound daily, and it recovered. But, magnificent animal as it was, it never seemed wholly to regain its wits. It allowed no one but the cook ever to touch it and would spit and snarl at anyone who came near it. Some evenings my father would steal down to the kitchen when the maids had gone to bed, and would try and woo it, to see if he could stroke it. Slowly he used to get his hand within a foot of it, while it glared at him malevolently, then just as success appeared within reach, it would turn on him and threaten to attack him.

Grumbling a little, Alice brought me an armful of paper and wood and a little paper bag with two or three potatoes in it. She stuffed a box of matches in my pocket.

'Don't blame me if you're ill, then,' she said, 'proper indigestion you'll get.'

I seized my booty and ran into the garden, across the wet lawn, past the great chestnut tree, past the old dark summer house. It cherished secrets, carved inside on the dark wooden walls, for here generations of Victorian lovers had chiselled out hearts, framing their initials. I always wondered if anyone would ever carve a heart for me.

I threaded my way through the bushes of the shrubbery, found a little open space, and prepared my fire. The mist cleared a little and the sun fell caressingly on my face. I was gazing over the great mountains of the Rockies, blue in the morning haze. My horse was tethered at my side, cropping the coarse sweet wild grass.

In an open space I knelt and, fumblingly, prepared my fire. A little flame trickled up the paper onto the sticks. Dear heaven, it was alight! I gathered an armful of twigs and put my potatoes in the tiny pile of ashes. I wrinkled my nose with pleasure as the smoke twisted a little fitfully into the cool morning air. For a long time I stayed there, chewing the slightly softened exterior of my potatoes, whose insides were still marble-hard. Although they tasted of nothing but ash, they were sweet to me.

A loud cry came from the house. Someone was shouting my name again and again. A rude reality broke in and I ran indoors.

'Where *have* you been? It's time for prayers, we are all waiting for you. Get out of those now, quickly.' My governess was chattering on.

I ran up the stairs, laid my lovely Red Indian suit on a chair, brushed my hair, washed quickly and ran down again, to take my seat in the dining room where the whole household was assembled—not too pleased at being kept waiting.

My father gazed at me benignly. 'I am going to read your birthday Psalm today. Psalm 121,' he said. His voice was firm and pleasant. There was a gladness in it when he read the Bible.

'I will lift up mine eyes unto the hills, from whence cometh my help.

My help cometh from the Lord which made heaven and earth.' The room was full of peace and calm as the beautiful words rose and fell, and the mountains were stretching away before my eyes.

His voice stopped, and the family, in one unified movement, swept onto its knees. I was barely conscious of them, for my spirit was wandering, far and free.

.   .   .   .   .

While I was still a small girl, two of my father's older sisters died. The first to go was my Aunt Mary, a widow whose invalid husband had been dead for some years. She lived in the ground floor flat in a dark gloomy pillared Georgian house.

Aunt Mary had an almost jealous affection for me. She was rather a passionate person of extreme respectability, who often failed to get on with her other sisters who were inclined to dominate her. I would visit her from time to time. As soon as I pressed the bell the door would be flung open and I would be swamped in a bony embrace.

'My dearest, most favourite niece', she would cry. She would make little suppers à deux, having asked what I wanted some days previously. My choice was unambitious, and always the same—Heinz tomato soup which had not long been on the market, and especially fat juicy sausages from a local manufacturer.

Together we would perch on hard wooden chairs in her little drab kitchen which faced the street, the sausages sizzling pleasantly in the frying-pan, the gathering darkness outside pressing on the big old-fashioned window panes, while a single shaft of light from a street gas lamp outside fell across the corner of the kitchen table. My aunt would rock steadily to and fro telling me of her sorrows and loneliness and of past happiness when her husband was alive.

She had a little drawing room, stuffy and hermetically sealed, where she kept the faded treasures of her married life. She almost never used this room; the cream window blinds, which were pulled up and down by a cord with a little wooden acorn at the end, were kept perpetually half drawn. Sometimes I played little tunes on her piano, whose muffled damp keys must never have been tuned. Sometimes I fingered through her old-fashioned Victorian books, but found little to my taste. She was surrounded by an atmosphere of such enclosed loneliness that it shocked me. Like Queen Victoria, she appeared to be in mourning for life. She always wore black clothes, a neat but shapeless black dress indoors, with a white modesty vest at the neck, and outdoors a long black coat with a large black fur collar and a voluminous hat, swathed in black silk. Her auburn hair, fast turning into white, was piled in a bun high on the back of her head.

In her last illness, she fell into a sort of semi-coma for almost a year and my father arranged for a retired trained nurse to live with her and care for her. Sometimes I would visit her, and creep quietly in to sit by the bed. While the nurse would busy herself making little drinks to feed to her with a teaspoon, I would hold her hand which lay, almost as if it did not belong to her, on the eiderdown. As I sat there, the very young with the prematurely old, I felt a deep pity for this human wreck. I would grip her hand the harder, just to reassure her that another person was sitting beside her. The tired heavy eyes would slowly open, a momentary smile would pass across her face, and as swiftly go, and she would have slipped back into some far distant place where none could follow. Young as I was, I felt that her death was the freeing of a soul in prison.

It was arranged that her funeral should take place from our house. Some of my father's sisters belonged to the Church of England, but Aunt Mary was a Plymouth Sister. It says much for the family solidarity that a number of the more worldly and wealthy Anglican cousins in London, and beyond, made the journey to be present at her funeral.

The first part of the day was of unrelieved gloom, although a little trickle of excitement crept through me as my father's various cousins arrived. I hung over the mahogany banisters, gazing down from the third floor where I was supposed to remain in my nursery. I was watched over by the faded little woman who was known as my 'nursery governess'. She was totally ineffective and useless and had to take me out in the park every day near my home, among other tasks. Looking back, I cannot believe her life was rewarding in any way.

The first to arrive was Uncle Harry, a delightful wealthy banker, distinguished to look at, with thick silvery hair and white moustache, and a slightly crooked but interesting aquiline nose. He was immaculately dressed in Bond Street clothes. He was one of the Directors of the Bank in Fleet Street called Tellson's by Dickens in the *Tale of Two Cities*. He entered the house with a studied cheerfulness as if funerals were just necessary evils and must not be allowed to generate too much solemnity. Poor Mary had gone to her everlasting rest and this should be a cause for thankfulness.

His firm assured hand grip, humorous smile and wicked wink would be a relief to my mother I knew. He ran up the stairs quickly to see me for a few minutes. His cultured rather melodious deep voice, and the slight scent of the best pipe tobacco which lingered around him, made him especially interesting to me. He was my Godfather and the husband of one of my father's younger sisters, a charming, easy and kindly man; there was the deepest affection between my father and him. Whenever they met they clasped each other's hands, beaming at each other with love and tolerant appreciation, although they were entirely different in character and outlook.

My father's cousins, Fred and John, entered, brisk and genial men, very small in stature, with great dignity and courtesy. Cousin Fred had a small aristocratic face and an enormous moustache. He was a Major from the Boer and first World War, and now was quite a wealthy landowner, having founded an outstanding pedigree herd of Jersey cattle in Norfolk. Cousin John was a rosy little doctor, with a pink bald head fringed with silvery hair. His conversation was difficult and repetitive, and he had a slight stammer until he was at ease with you: 'Yes, yes, yes. Quite so . . . quite so . . . Dear me, dear me.' He was a widower with a very beautiful old house on the edge of one of Surrey's village greens. His servants were devoted to him, literally wrapping him in his overcoat and muffler each day before he set out on his daily rounds. His little elderly chauffeur, who accompanied him everywhere, was a man who had never learned to read or write in his life, yet whose natural gentlemanliness and sweetness of character were seen in all he did.

The other aunts arrived. There was murmuring and kissing in the hall, between them and my mother. Everyone trooped into the dining room where morning coffee was being served. A buzz of subdued conversation floated tantalisingly up the stairs.

All the navy blue blinds in the front of the house at every window were fully drawn. My nursery was fearful and gloomy, lit by the electric light in mid-morning. Gloomily I pressed one eye to the edge of the blind which I daringly lifted a fraction.

Cousin James was climbing out of a station cab. He entered the house at a brisk trot. If ever a figure stepped straight out of Charles Dickens, it was Cousin James. He had ruddy cheeks, great white beetling eyebrows, a piercing rather fierce expression, and enormous tufts of whisker which seemed to have got slightly misplaced, sprouting out of his nose. He was something of an original and, on his rare visits, rushed up to the nursery to discuss books and poetry and life. He would then write me long letters, which I was too young to understand, and would send me parcels of books to read.

Soon there was a muffled sound of horses' hoofs. Walking round the corner, with a man at their head, came the two glossy black horses drawing a hearse on which lay the flower-covered coffin. This was followed by a number of black horse-drawn cabs. The top-hatted leader of this equipage reverently approached the front door and rang the bell. The doors of the cabs were opened by each driver with precision, and the family issued out of the house, united in mourning the passing of one of their number. The men wore black top hats and frock coats; the women also wore un-relieved black. My mother, on whose shoulders had fallen the arrangements for her sister-in-law's funeral, emerged looking anxious and preoccupied; she turned from one to another of the relatives with some polite remark, indicating in which cab they would travel. The horses now and then stamped restlessly on the cobbled road, but at last all was ready. The doors shut, the relatives peered out through the glass side windows, and the procession started off slowly, the

cabs swaying from side to side with the slow movement of
the horses.

It was quite an impressive end for Aunt Mary, I thought,
as the black line of vehicles turned and wound away into the
distance; I could watch it getting steadily smaller, seen
through the massive tall trunks of the plane trees in front of
the houses, whose leaves were stirring in the west wind.
Then it turned a corner and was gone.

That evening the relatives had all departed except Uncle
Harry. His refreshing normality filled the house. He sat
relaxed in the drawing room, smoking his pipe—with my
mother's permission—gladly given, I fancy.

I crept up to him.

'Play to me, Uncle Harry', I begged. He winked mischievously, and rose.

'What shall it be then, Anne?', he said.

'Chu Chin Chow—please.'

Head flung back, pipe between his teeth, he poised his
elegant hands above the keys. Then the rousing gaiety of the
Robbers' Chorus filled the room. I hung over the piano in
admiration.

The day was ending better than it had begun, I thought.

6

WORLDLY ENCOUNTERS

EVERY Easter holidays my mother remarked that I looked a little 'peaky', and my father suggested that a few days at the sea would do me good. He would suggest that I should be taken to a quiet boarding-house at Weston-super-Mare, where the ozone was thought to be very bracing and beneficial. The solid rather Victorian boarding-house was very comfortably run. The guests were generally quiet middle-class people, often strong Nonconformists. Now and then, however, more unusual people stayed there, as I was to find out.

My father and mother were always given the largest and most comfortable bedroom, and were popular guests. I had a tiny room nearby and the breeze blowing off the sea rattled its window; the seaweedy smell drifting in stirred up a restless longing for adventure.

My spirits always rose at that first sight of the endless sands and mud under the wide, windy sky. I would race down to the shore, hair flying, sixpence—real wealth—clutched in my hand, to find the donkeys. They were always waiting for me and I would caress the velvet soft noses of Nell, Bessie and Primrose, and choose my mount for the day, and we would be off, hooves thumping, marking clearly our journey across the hard sand.

One Easter two men came to stay in the boarding-house. Instinctively I sensed that they were 'worldly' and different. One was tall and dark, wore loud tweeds and looked faintly raffish. The other, small and fair, suggested 'The Turf' to me, why, I find it hard to imagine, as my knowledge of 'The

51

Turf' must have been almost non-existent. One morning I was playing with my ball on the beach, throwing it up as high into the sky as I could and catching it again. I was surprised to see the two men strolling along and eyeing me appraisingly. The fair one stepped forward. A faint uneasiness seized me. I might have longings for the world, but not, I thought, for their world.

'May I join you?' he said. I was astonished. The ball game became fast and furious. He tested me out with hard demanding throws and catches for some time. Then, turning to my mother, who was by now standing near, he said, 'I have never seen a straighter eye in my life.' Now it was my turn to look appraising. What could he be after? He requested my mother's permission to teach me golf on the sands next morning. However, although he arrived with several golf clubs and effusive promises of my undoubted skill, I am afraid I was a disappointment. My straight eye must have had an off-day, or else golf was decidedly not my game. However, I was flattered at being the object of attention.

The next day I was intrigued and excited to hear various whisperings and consultations between the kindly proprietors, now looking anxious, and my parents. Something unusual was evidently afoot, and my new found 'friend' had mysteriously vanished, together with his companion. A policeman later arrived. It transpired that the two men were not all they seemed, and had left after forging a 'dud' cheque in payment of their account. The world really was intruding on my ordered life. I felt it was an unusual experience for the daughter of a Plymouth brother to have played with a crook! My heart swelled with pride at the thought of the story I would tell in school.

Another year a different sort of guest arrived. He was a small, elderly man with a mop of soft white hair and gold-rimmed spectacles, behind which he looked now penetratingly at one, now into the distance, often with a sparkle of child-like pleasure at what he saw. Mr. Considine was a real musician, I discovered. Every evening when the respectable company were gathered in the drawing-room with their embroidery or knitting,—'lounges' being then rooms reserved only for smokers—one lady or another would beg him to play. Then the piano came alive, I would feel an itch in my feet, my toes and fingers would start to tap and I fretted at the stillness and intentness of the adult listeners.

One day it was raining. Afternoon tea on trolleys had been removed from the room by the amiable old-fashioned bespectacled maid, in the traditional cap with two white streamers down the back. By chance I was alone in the room, curled up reading on the rather gloomily coloured green plush sofa. I gazed through the long white lace curtains, looped back, past the aspidistra on its stand, and a depression of dullness engulfed me. I hardly noticed little Mr. Considine step quietly in and take his seat on the piano stool. But the music began. I forgot my surroundings. The music seemed to flood through me, gayer and faster, and quite unconsciously, I think, I began to dance, in a natural instinctive way, just as the music spoke to me. It was my companion, playmate, laughing, mocking, taking me by the hand. An overwhelming happiness seized me as I moved and turned and glided in time to the rhythm. Time stood still, for I had vanished into some enchanted land.

The music stopped suddenly as the door opened and my mother came in. I was conscious of a faint look of surprise on her face. A horrible realisation of what I had been doing seized me, and I stood blushing and hanging my head.

'I wonder if you know that your little girl is a natural dancer', Mr. Considine was saying. 'She moves with the music in a way I have not seen before. This is a real gift. I do hope you will let her take this up.' I was filled with horror.

E

Dancing was forbidden by the Plymouth Brethren; certainly attendance at dances was, because unsuitable if not actually sinful desires might be aroused. We were never allowed to learn the formal ballroom dances, although physical education was encouraged as being healthy.

What errant streak possessed me so that I had this overwhelming desire to fling myself into the joys of the music? My poor mother, secretly I believe in sympathy with me, was in a quandary. She made evasive answers, but Mr. Considine was pressing. It was clear he must not enter into conversation with my father. I do not remember any conclusion she came to, except that she always encouraged me to do all the country dancing in the school curriculum.

This deep desire for a spontaneous gaiety fought in me with an equally profound wish for a faith as real as my father's. The two nearly tore me apart. The story in the Gospels of the lost sheep, and the ninety and nine who were safe, sometimes moved me secretly to tears. I had no doubt I was that lost one, and I longed for the Shepherd to seek me out, for often I felt it was I away on the dark mountain-side, and I longed to be brought in to the warmth and safety of the fold.

.   .   .   .   .

I was about twelve years old when I experienced what was to me a significant encounter at this same boarding-house.

An elderly couple with a large chauffeur-driven car came to stay for a short holiday, bringing a young grandson, about a year older than me. He was a fair, pleasant-looking boy, I thought, and I admired the dark navy blue suit and Eton collar he wore on the Sunday. I was not particularly interested in boys except as creatures whose games and ideas seemed far more exciting and sensible than girls'; for most girls' games and occupations, dolls, sewing, cooking, seemed

boring and trivial to me. Shyly, we smiled at each other. I
hoped I would be allowed to play with him. We must have
gone off on the donkeys together and played on the beach,
for I remember that the games were exciting and I was happy.

On his last day we were sitting under a large flowering
tree in the garden, whose branches drooped towards the
ground making a sort of natural secret tent. We talked happily.

'May I write to you when I get home?' he said, gravely
courteous.

'Why, of course', I said, secretly surprised and gratified.

'Will you write to me, too?' he said.

'Yes, I will', I answered, thinking that this would be
something to look forward to. I loved letters. I remember he
lived in Solihull. I told my parents about his interesting wish.
To my horror and surprise, a serious view was taken of this.
I was told that we knew nothing about him or his parents
and that I must not write. A secret desolation enfolded me.
I would be unable to keep my word. He was obviously 'in the
world' and not for me.

Every summer we went away again. My mother had to
organise a major operation to shut up our house for my
father's annual three weeks holiday in August. The campaign
began at Easter when my parents visited various quiet sea-
side resorts and chose apartments which were reserved for
them. This meant taking the whole of a house, whose owner
would cook for and look after us. But for a number of years
we had been going now to South Devon.

The manner of my parents' discovery of this house was
typical. That year one or two patients were critically ill and
my father felt unable to make plans to go away and leave
them. In spite of this, my mother had to arrange to let the
maids go away on a certain date and to close the house.
August drew near and still nothing was decided. Dark com-

plaints began issuing from the kitchen. My father still vacillated.

'Do not worry, Lou, the Lord will provide a holiday for us in his own good time.'

'But I must let the maids go, and shut the house.'

The days passed and now it was a week before the holiday. My mother was harassed, my father seraphic, in hourly anticipation of guidance. 'Well, WHAT are we to do?' my mother pressed again for an answer. Being practical, she knew that it would be extremely difficult to get any accommodation by now, and they never went to large hotels, whose atmosphere they found unsympathetic.

'Well,' said my father brightly, 'we will just pray about it then, and commit this matter to the Lord.' In this my father was logical, for as his life was God-centred, he believed that he could therefore rely on God's help in even the smallest detail of living. Forthwith, therefore, he knelt down at the dining-room table, with my mother, and asked the Lord to direct them as to what must be done in the matter of the summer holiday. On rising from his knees he seized *The Times* newspaper and his eyes immediately fell on an advertisement for apartments to let, through a cancellation, in a small South Devon fishing village. Although the advertisement said 'no children' my father said, 'I believe that is where we must go.' And so it was to be. We went there for thirteen years in succession, and my parents were never happier than when they lived quietly there, completely relaxed and at peace, away from all their many responsibilities.

Mrs. Chown, who cooked for us and looked after us, was a remarkable monumental figure. She was never seen to leave the house, as her husband—a little gnarled man, kindly and silent—did any necessary errands. Her stories of the early days of her life were incredible to me, as she had been one of twenty-three children.

I remember that among certain friends who visited us here for afternoon tea was a distinguished couple, deeply courteous Plymouth Brethren, rather of my parents' calibre, I thought. These were Colonel and Mrs. George Wingate, parents of Brigadier Orde Wingate of the Burma Campaign in World War II, himself brought up in the same tradition as I was. It was a gently happy tea-party. These cultured people all had, to use a word that is almost derogatory nowadays, a 'purity' of outlook and a steadfast hope in their faith that gave them a special calmness and serenity. It is interesting now to read in Christopher Sykes' well-known biography of Brigadier Wingate, the assessment of his Puritan upbringing. After describing the extreme strictness of his home, he goes on to say, 'It is also certainly true that from the world of piety and sincerity and submission to the Divine Will, where his parents had their being, he drew strength for the rest of his life.' I could add that those who try to comprehend the Brethren home seen at its best in those days, cannot imagine the innocent gaiety and simple loving kindness of its setting. The tensions began when it was necessary to emerge into the world.

South Devon was a great joy to my father. After a brisk, brief bathe each morning, he would often walk the mile or so to the rocks jutting out into the sea at one end of the bay, where there were hundreds of small deep rock pools. Here, with his pocket magnifying glass and a shrimping net, and his peaked cloth holiday cap back to front on his head, he would lie or squat by the hour, examining tiny creatures in the pools and watching their habits. Sometimes he would catch them in the net and place them gently in a small metal bucket. These would be taken back to our lodgings for more detailed study, perhaps under the microscope which he always brought with him. Next day they would be replaced in their pool.

Sunday mornings in Devon followed the same pattern as at home. A little red brick hall was the place of worship for the Brethren, who were fairly numerous as this was near their place of origin. It was mainly a gathering of homely, devout fisher folk, with perhaps one or two clerks and some retired businessmen. The arrival of 'Doctor' in their midst was a cause for simple and touching pleasure. They wrung his hand, pumping it up and down, their rosy, outdoor faces glowing. They looked to him for new inspiration and help, and he was always invited to take the Gospel Meeting in the evening. This consisted of an evangelistic appeal to the un-saved, after hymns and the reading of Scripture. However, the congregation generally consisted entirely of the elect and no-one was likely to need this specific exhortation—unless, perhaps, any children had 'made no profession'—that is of conversion. The changed life before and after one became a Christian was very real to these fishermen. So they felt they must cast the Gospel net further. Every Sunday evening in the summer months they held an open-air service on the beach.

Now my mother had some London friends from her student days staying near us, scintillating, interesting people, I thought, and I knew they thought the Plymouth Brethren odd. So I kept very quiet about our Sunday routine. One Sunday the elders of the Meeting asked my father to speak at the open-air beach service that evening. I was filled with horror and dismay. He would be seen in public, exposed and vulnerable, preaching about his faith, which I knew meant so much to him; if our 'worldly' friends saw him they would secretly laugh at him and think him eccentric. In imagina-tion, I pictured their reactions, and it was unbearable. But when he asked me to go with him I felt my courage, which was little, ebb away to nothing. This was too much. Nervous and totally withdrawn—a non-participator—I stood on the extreme perimeter of the little group, as they stood on the stony, curving shore, the red cliffs sheltering the bay, the waves splashing gently behind them and the setting sun bathing the headland in a soft, golden light. Just as in Galilee, it was a group of simple fishermen who gathered there to speak of their Master. Suntanned holidaymakers passed to and fro, glancing at them only momentarily.

My father stepped forward quietly, to tell of what it meant to him to be a Christian. Grave, sad, eloquent, he looked at me and I felt my rebellious attitude was like a stab in the back to him who gave me nothing but love. Why could I never reconcile this side of my life with the everyday secular one? Yet I believed that one day I must find a faith that would have to mean all or nothing.

Next morning on the beach one of my mother's friends said suddenly to me, 'I hear your father was preaching on the beach last night.' A deep blush crept over my face. Was she privately mocking my father? I could not bear it. I was withdrawing rapidly, an anguish in my mind. We belonged nowhere, we were outcasts, people to be laughed at as odd; queer people no-one would want as friends. She spoke again, turning to look at me with a penetrating glance.

'I think that was splendid. Do you realise that your father is a very brave man?' The slow, hard tears gathered in my eyes and I turned away quickly. There was nothing I could say.

7

A MERRY HEART

IF he did not approve of dancing, my father had many other pleasures to put in its place, for he was a profoundly happy man. I do not think I ever once heard him complain or grumble. His real love for his Creator had given him a love for the Creation, from every bird, beast and flower, down to the tiniest insect or sea creature in a rock pool. He had a vast knowledge of natural history and kept neatly written detailed accounts about any interesting find or discovery or natural event.

One evening he tiptoed into my room, agog with boyish excitement, 'Keep quiet, Anne,' he said, gripping my wrist as he drew me into his dressing-room, where he proceeded to pull on thick, leather gloves.

I tiptoed after him and followed his gaze to the top of a bookcase. His bookcases were full of books of evangelical theology, the New Testament and the Greek Septuagint, copies of the Hebrew Old Testament, almost every known translation of the Bible in every size, jostling together with the latest medical books, copies of the British Medical Journal and the Lancet, with a few surprising oddments like *The Woman in White* by Wilkie Collins and *The Life of Lord George Sanger*—of Sanger's Circus. It was not a book I had to look at, however. Perched on top of the highest bookcase, glaring and winking in a totally unembarrassed but rather annoyed manner, sat a large, brown owl. My father's joy knew no bounds.

'We must catch him and put him out of the window', he said. Indeed, the flapping blind, half drawn, and open window, whose curtains were blowing in the strong wind, showed how he had got in. Climbing on a chair, my father approached the bird. The owl did not wish to be set free, it seemed. It flapped heavily onto the top of a tallboy. I was despatched for the wooden steps. No sooner had my father climbed to the top of these and leaned forward to clasp the bird, than it flew on to the curtain rail and gazed at us malevolently. The steps were moved on, the process was repeated round and round the room. It took a very long time to free the owl, but my father was indefatigable and had a way of handling birds and beasts when no-one else could.

On another occasion my mother was troubled by a mouse in the bedroom. My father was asked to despatch it. He produced a box-type trap, which quickly did its work. The lively mouse sat inside the trap peering out with beady, bright eyes, where it was later discovered by my mother. Quickly she seized the bedroom speaking tube. This was a fascinating object, into whose mahogany funnel-shaped mouth you could halloo downstairs to the hall or kitchens, the sound reverberating out at the other end as a sort of loud, agitated howl. On hearing this downstairs, you seized the other end of the tube, which had a similar speaking funnel, and a thin and faint conversation could then be carried on between those at the top and those at the bottom of the house. My mother hallooed, was answered, and requested that the mouse be immediately removed and despatched. The tube went lifeless. After a short period, she picked up the trap distastefully and with a certain marked annoyance, descended four long flights of stairs to the hall and placed trap and contents on the hall table. The front door opened and shut. My father never came upstairs, no sound was heard below. Half an hour—an hour—passed. My mother grew anxious. Eventually a soft step was heard—my father was quietly creeping up the stairs.

'What have you done with the mouse?' asked my mother suspiciously. There was a long pause.

'He was really an enchanting little mouse, so intelligent,' said my father evasively.

'WHAT did you do with him?'

'Oh, well, I took him out for a walk, quite a long way from here, and let him go free!' My father was certainly the kindest-hearted of men and would go to endless trouble to help and heal animals and birds as well as men.

When I was about fourteen years old there was an unusual saga with the rooks, who each Spring nested in the great plane trees opposite our house. Each year we counted the completed nests, and the rookery would generally consist of about eight to ten nests. But very often in the Spring gales a nest would become dislodged and would fall to the ground. My father would take us out to study it, and once, to my mother's dismay, brought one into the house on the largest tin tray available. Of immense span, often four to six feet in diameter from the outermost stout twigs, it would sometimes still have eggs in it.

One year there was an unusually raucous and agitated cawing from the rooks. My father, whose ear was attuned to any unusual sound from the birds, left his work and ran outside. There on the ground was not only a nest, but a terrified baby rook, whose parents had set up a frenzied squawking. Back went my father for the thick, leather gloves. In a minute he had gently gripped the baby and brought it indoors. My mother and the parlourmaid showed consternation, but he carried it through the door at the back of the house, down the steep steps to the garden, into an enclosed yard adjoining the second basement at the back of the house. Within a few hours a joiner had been summoned and had successfully erected a large cage of wire netting with perches and a large box nest for the bird to live in. Meanwhile, the

parent rooks located their young one and flew unusually near
the house to the very edge of the yard, calling their distress.
Now came the problem of feeding this demanding little
creature. My father, to the cook's annoyance, ordered three
meals a day to be sent up from the kitchen on a little tray;
these were brought up by Gladys or Lucy: bread and milk
for breakfast, a boiled egg—rather oddly—for lunch, and
bread and butter for tea. Then, with a long pronged piece
of wood which he had fashioned, my father would descend
to the yard with a camp stool and the tray of food. There he
would sit and feed the rook with morsels off the stick. He
talked to it gently and caressingly all the time and soon the
rook grew to love him as its parent. Every day when my
father's car stopped at the front door the rook started to utter
its shrill cry and hop excitedly on the perch. It never uttered
a sound for any other car, and this was on the other side of
the house. We always knew when my father had arrived at
the front door by the rook's call.

After this had gone on two or three months, my father left
the large door of the cage open. Soon Pippo, as he was called,
began to hop in and out of the cage to the garden. Slowly
and heavily at first, he clumsily tried his wings, and eventually
flew onto a low branch of the chestnut tree. At first he came
back regularly to the cage after a short period of exercise, and
went on being fed by my father. But one day he flew high up
into the chestnut tree and vanished. My father was much
saddened until a great uproar was heard at the very top of
the house. Pippo had arrived at the window of our attic
bathroom and was sitting on the windowsill demanding food.
For many days my father made his pilgrimage upstairs to
feed the rook at the bathroom window. Sometimes Pippo
entered the room, and once fell in the bath. This went on
until it was time to go away to Devon on our annual holiday.
My father would hardly go. At last arrangements were made

for some one to come in and feed the rook and my father was persuaded to leave home. To his grief, my father found that the rook did not like his new benefactor, and after a few days he never came back.

Fortunately there was a happy ending to this story. While walking through the park one late summer evening when our holiday was over, my father and I heard a commotion above us, and a young rook flew down onto a low branch of a tree just above the path where we were walking. It was Pippo, and I do not know who was the more delighted at the re-union. After this there was often a meeting in the park, Pippo following my father from tree to tree, calling to him. Then one day Pippo brought a young female rook with him to show my father, who was enchanted to see that the bird was not alone any more.

I still have photographs which bring back the memory of this unusual story of a rare friendship between a man and a bird.

.   .   .   .   .

Although my life was, perhaps, limited in one direction, there were many opportunities for amusement and initiative in another. My father possessed the Victorian love of prac-tical jokes, and indeed, even in later life could not resist from time to time playing some trick on the family. I remember that one Christmas Day we were seated around the dining table, as usual, various elderly or lonely relatives with us. Now, my father possessed a most diabolical small electric shock machine, used on sufferers from rheumatism.

'Will you be so kind as all to take hands?' he said, after the turkey and Christmas pudding had departed. 'I have a little experiment which I know will interest you'. We all held hands around the table, while the two at the head of the table had to place their free hand on a small handle, one at each side of the box. Surreptitiously my father began to wind a third little handle. All our hands locked together! We were, in truth, electrified, no-one being able to let go of her neighbour, while an unpleasant mild electric shock ran through all our arms.

'So good and invigorating for you', he would say blandly, gazing at the ceiling, while my aunts screamed, my mother remonstrated and then fell to rating him. Rocking with mirth, he would continue to wind the handle until we were all crying for mercy. His pleasure was so acute that he could hardly be persuaded to release us.

I think I inherited this love of jokes from him. Life could be made so much more lively. I found that one of my Aunts, a Plymouth sister, was very gullible in the matter of receiving letters. So once I concocted a letter in a forged hand asking her to speak at a mythical Women's Meeting at a certain place and time. Her agitation at not knowing the writer or the proposed place of meeting, and on finding the address rather illegible, knew no bounds. She chattered on in perplexity and indecision for fully half an hour, asking my father's advice, He had quickly guessed the origin of the letter and his refusal to advise her threw her into a rage and she accused him of being very unfeeling. I hardly dared to reveal the truth in the end, and she would scarcely speak to me for some time.

Soon after this I discovered another interest. Always anxious for some little excitement, I took to filling in forms in magazines for free samples. Interesting little parcels of face cream, a luxury indeed, toothpaste, soap, and even lipstick,—carefully hoarded and hidden away—now began to arrive, and my appetite was aroused. I became more ambitious. I ordered the Encyclopedia Brittanica on approval, 'No obligation to buy' and various other books. A car laden with all its volumes, and many others, arrived from some distance, ready to disgorge its contents. It arrived, unforgivably, during consulting hours. The man made a scene on the step and would not depart. The parlourmaid had to summon my father from his patients. He was seized with a rare anger at being disturbed. Worse was to follow. The very next day a van arrived from a long distance with a very large refrigerator. This was carried into the house. Again, the traveller was insistent that it had been ordered, and would not depart. Again my father had to be summoned. Hanging over the banisters, listening to the angry argument in the hall, I realised that my only hope lay in a speedy retreat. I flew into the garden and climbed quickly up the tallest tree, well away from the house, and thought it wise not to appear again for a very long time.

Fortunately for me, for else I might have been a very lonely child, I had certain friends who were also brought up strictly and who accepted my background without surprise or comment. One friend, Joyce, was born the day before me. She was one of three children, having an older and younger brother. She had also numerous aunts and uncles, and cousins of about our age, and I used to spend the weekend at her home from time to time. They were memorable days. Together we would concoct elaborate games of hilarious make-believe, and our escapades were the despair of her kind-hearted mother. Her grandfather, the Mayor of the city, lived in a beautiful ivy-covered mansion set in a very large garden which offered endless possibilities to his numerous grandchildren, some of whom were always to be found playing in it. He had had iron steps built around one large tree, curving around the great trunk and leading up into a sort of tree house with a circle of seats and a wooden floor. Here plans of campaign and secret discussions were thrashed out on hot summer days, while from our high perch we watched the heat haze lying heavy over the City beneath us, for the house was set on a great hillside. I remember the Union Jack

on the massive flagstaff, dominating the edge of the garden,—
which fell in a precipice drop to houses far away beneath,—
stirring gently to and fro with the suggestion of a rising breeze.
Several summerhouses were secreted around the garden,
and, with Joyce's younger brother roped in for our endless
games, we embarked on great dramas of rescue, disaster,
thrill and mystery—or home-making.

One day, up the tree, our brains teeming with almost too
many ideas to fulfil, I said, 'Let's dress up in your mother's
old clothes and pretend we are collecting for a new home to
be built for the blind. We'll have a book of subscribers and
we'll "take in" all your relations.' Swiftly we ran back to
Joyce's house and were pleased to find her mother was out
shopping. We ransacked her wardrobe. Our histrionic talent
must have been fairly developed, for by the time we had
finished our amateur make-up we appeared as two ageing
spinsters in large black floppy hats and with long dark dresses.
I shall never forget the walk to Joyce's grandfather's house,
through a busy shopping centre, eyeing passers-by, some of
whom knew us, to see if we were recognised. Apparently we
were not. We went up the Mayor's long drive. On ringing
the bell we asked the maid if we might see him on urgent
business. She eyed us piercingly, but without recognition. In
a moment he was with us, holding the arm of his kindly
wife, for he was near-sighted.

'Who are these people, Lucy?' he asked, peering at us.
In a somewhat quavery voice I described the plight of the
blind of the City and announced that the new building was
nearly completed.

'Well, I do NOT understand why I have been told nothing
about this, Lucy,' he said with annoyance. The interview
progressed. In a cracked voice Joyce explained it was a new
venture, and produced the cash book, neatly written up with
a list of supposed contributions from real and fictitious

characters. He studied it critically. But at this point his wife had recognised us and started trying to muffle her laughter in a handkerchief. Astounded, he turned to her, thunderous, thinking she was guilty of discourtesy to these faded women.

'Do you not recognise these ladies, dearest?' she asked. (His nickname in the family had become 'Dearest' as she always called him this.)

'No, I do NOT, Lucy, and I do not understand what the matter is.' He produced five shillings and handed it to us. By this time we ourselves were overcome and could not speak, and he became even more irritable and confused, and so at last we revealed our identity.

'God bless my soul, Lucy,' he said with a great reverberating bellow of laughter, 'I couldn't have believed it.' And he embraced us both, tickling us with his thick beard and saying we were to keep the money.

Our day was a sort of triumphal progress. We went from one relative to another. None of them knew us. By the time we returned home it was evening, and Joyce's mother was looking out for us. We turned in at the gate, two thin black figures with beatific expressions.

'*Joyce! Anne! what* your *father* would say, I simply *cannot imagine!*' She always talked, delightfully, in italics. The sight of us, as usual, melted her annoyance at our lateness, she was overcome with laughter and kissed us both in relief at seeing us, and exasperation.

Years later, Joyce was to marry one of Britain's most famous scientists, knighted for his outstanding work. She had a family of five children. I often wonder if our children ever have quite the same fun and hilarity as we did. Because for children who were strictly brought up, we could be carefree and happy in an entirely uninhibited way, and yet it was a simple spontaneous gaiety, springing up from nothing except light hearts and our own unfettered imagination.

8

THE SPELL OF LONDON

MY mother lived a separate life of the spirit, I am sure, unfettered by the limits and confines of Brethren life and theology. In her heart she was still the Vicar's daughter, noted in her father's diary for her kindness, but sharing the gaiety which characterised her brother. Her father had been broadminded and humane, devoted to his family and seeing that they enjoyed a happy life. As a child she had been taken to parties, dancing classes, concerts, the theatre, the Lord Mayor's Show; there were visits to the Boat Race, the Crystal Palace, and all the wonders of late Victorian London.

She knew well how bitterly I felt being deprived of activities and entertainments allowed to my friends, and went out of her way to arrange every expedition and outing that could possibly be undertaken within my father's rules. If he was doubtful she often reasoned gently with him, and permission for this or that activity would be granted. I was regularly taken to concerts, but particularly loved dramatic impersonations in song by that fascinating singer of the 1920's, Jean Sterling MacKinlay, who could transform herself from one character to another with perhaps a scarf or a hat and whose warmth and vitality charmed her audiences. Remarkably enough, I remember a red-letter day in my life when my mother took me to a circus. My father, with his passion for animals, owned a book, *The Life of Lord George Sanger*, which described this great old circus owner and his humane approach to the training of his animals. Sanger's Circus came to Bath and my father could not resist this. I was despatched with his blessing and on our return he could not hear enough about every thrill, every act. Wistfully, through our eyes, the boy in him listened agog, laughing at the antics of the clowns, his sense of the ridiculous always ready to appear. Next day he went down to see all the animals. This small treat meant so much to him, for he enjoyed everything he did to the full. I am sure I felt more keenly than he ever did how much he had given up. I knew his sense of fun was strong, there was so much he could have enjoyed. However, he was conscious of no deprivation. He lived in the spirit of John Bunyan's shepherd boy:

> 'I am content with what I have
> Little be it or much,
> And, Lord, contentment still I crave
> Because thou savest such.'

There was another vexed question when I was a child. The wireless had just made its appearance. It was regarded by many religious people with suspicion. Unsuitable, if not actually harmful, opinions were voiced through it. I once heard an eccentric elderly lady remark that she would find it impossible to own one, as it was surely a demonic device, for was not Satan the Prince of the power of the air? My mother quietly bided her time. After a long period, by which time most of our friends now owned the fascinating 'box', she was rewarded for her patience in an odd way. One of my step-sisters had an accident while teaching. A heavy blackboard slipped and crashed on to her toes and broke them. She had to stay in bed for some time, her feet in plaster. Impatient and vigorous, appalled at a long spell of inactivity, she was not the best of patients. By some herculean— and subtle—effort, my mother persuaded my father to hire a wireless, to help entertain her. I shall never forget how we all crouched around it, enchanted, listening to its screeches, whistles—and music. That was the end of the veto on the wireless. It saved her sanity, and ours.

Once or twice a year my mother would arrange an expedition to London to go shopping and to visit her first love, the British Museum. Here, with deep absorption, she studied the wonderful finds of Leonard, later Sir Leonard Woolley, and Sir Flinders Petrie, in Ur of the Chaldees and other Bible lands; and then she would write articles on archaeology. On one occasion she took me to one of Sir Flinders Petrie's public lectures in University College. That magnificent old patriarchal Jew was still full of vigour. To me he seemed a reincarnation of Abraham with his noble head and flowing beard. A group of tall, slender, cultured young Jewesses came in to listen to him that day. I gazed at their graceful walk, their superb carriage, their regular chiselled features. Brought up on the Old Testament as much as the New, I seemed to be seeing an apotheosis of beauty; God's creation at its most compelling. I have often felt that the Jew, at his best, is unmatched. To me it was never 'odd' that the Jews were the chosen people.

On her museum marathons, I would trail after her, picking up sundry bits of information and knowledge, and collecting historical postcards. I came to have an entirely unmerited reputation at school for a vast general knowledge because at a very early age I had been able to enlighten a mistress as to the identity of Nefertiti of the wonderful profile. I had explained among other facts, how she was the mother-in-law of King Tutankamen.

We had a nice taste in restaurants. I remember a sparkling fountain in the middle of a vast, gold-pillared room, soft red carpets and exotic dishes, the setting made perfect by a gay, red-coated orchestra. This was entirely after my own heart.

Then once a year in the summer my mother would take me with her to visit London friends. She was well-known in the educational world and one of her chief interests was her work as governor of many schools. We used often to stay with a charming and cultured friend, Lady Savory, who was on the council of the Girls' Public School Trust, which governs many of England's leading girls' High Schools. Here, making myself inconspicuous, I used to listen to sparkling conversation among talented, gifted people. I remember Lady Magnus, wife of Sir Laurie Magnus, Chairman of the Girls' Public Day School Trust; she was a most delightful, gracious and beautiful Jewish lady. Another time we were summoned to tea with the Dowager Countess of Carlisle. This was the first house I had ever been in where a butler opened the door and showed us upstairs. Tea was informal, easy and friendly, her grandchildren sprawling on rugs on the floor.

Lady Savory's husband, Sir Joseph Savory, had been Lord Mayor of London, and we went on special visits to see the Guildhall and Mansion House. It was a world remote from my own, but fascinating. Photos of Queen Mary, ('With love from Mary R'), stood on beautiful glass-fronted book-cases and cabinets. Lady Savory and my mother shared a deep and sincere faith. I have never forgotten her patience and kindness to a small, lonely girl. Knowing my father's rules, she made special arrangements for many permissible forms of entertainment. One of my favourite expeditions was to take long rides on the Tube and Metropolitan Railway. I can still smell their delicious stuffy 'London' smell and remember how the thrill of the unfamiliar spelled happiness and romance to me. Then we once went to the vast pano-rama of *Hiawatha* in the Albert Hall, that magnificent singer, Stiles Allen, taking the part of old Nokomis.

Most wonderful of all to me were visits to Madame Tus-saud's and to Maskelyne's Theatre, which was the nearest I got to the live stage. This enchanting children's theatre, which gave the finest performances of magic and conjuring ever conceived, held me spellbound. First I fell in love with handsome, urbane Jasper Maskelyne in his dress suit and tails, with his dazzling charm. But even he was outshone for me by a devastatingly blue-eyed young man, with the gayest of smiles, who was fastened and tied up in silver chains, and after wonderful contortions freed himself. I still remember the dazzling, silvery spotlight with a slight haze of dust particles eddying in it, a sort of fairy mist dancing in front of the stage.

In the evening, dinner at the tall house in Onslow Square, was a formal affair, where I had to learn how to negotiate the mysteries of finger-bowls by sedulously watching—from under lowered eyelashes—the other sophisticated guests. Occasionally, I even made a small foray into the conversation: one evening the names of two prominent men in the world of education cropped up. It was found that my mother had known them well in her youth and had even lodged in the same house as one of them. This was a side of her life I had never pictured. Another name was mentioned and I gazed at her quizzically. 'And was he *another* man that you lived with?' The prolonged laughter seemed to suggest that I had made a witty remark. I could not imagine why, but it was quite gratifying. I suddenly noticed that my mother, flushed and sparkling, a fresh rose pinned becomingly into the folds of her graceful black evening gown, looked a different person. It was rather odd.

These were happy days. I was for ever waiting for the next excitement to come round the corner, and lived in a dreamy state of wondering what wonderful thing a day would bring forth.

My mother was always determined that I should receive the best possible education. Distinguished academic as she was, she seemed unperturbed that I showed no signs of her brilliance, and, on the whole, I remained obstinately pedestrian. I was, however, always stimulated by her presence, happy to listen to her intelligent conversation, to laugh with her at funny episodes, and to share small pleasures with her. For a woman with such a swift, sparkling intellect, and an almost masculine grasp of facts and figures and situations, political or domestic, she was quite remarkably simple and contented at heart.

From time to time she would slip quietly into my room and say with a merry look, 'Daddy thinks we should go out for the day. You have been working hard this week. It will do us good.' So, off we would go together on some small expedition, perhaps to take photos of the lovely Somerset countryside and gardens; perhaps to wander happily through the past, as it were, at Glastonbury and Wells; or to ride on a rattling, swaying tram to the outskirts of the City and have a picnic in the violet-starred woods of springtime. Best of all, we regularly returned to London, over the years, for the ostensible reason of broadening my education, but chiefly, I believe, for the acute pleasure it gave us both. Here we visited all the great Museums and the splendid institutions of England—The Houses of Parliament, Westminster Abbey, St. Paul's. Here I was fascinated by the Tower of London. It cast a spell over me. Imagination caught fire, as England in retrospect, was held in a microcosm in the colourful figures of the Beefeaters. I heard in imagination the shouts of crowds watching the executions, the sad cries of prisoners in the Tower, the hoarse voices of the guards. The words of Sir Walter Raleigh spoke to me, and I felt pressing in the deep sorrow of humanity:

> 'Even such is Time which takes in trust
> Our youth, our joys, our all we have,
> And pays us but with earth and dust;
> Who, in the dark and silent grave,

When we have wandered all our ways,
Shuts up the story of our days.
But from this earth, this grave, this dust,
My God shall raise me up I trust.'

These words spoke to me. I was growing up, and the idea of time and history and the passing of the years caused a great and clouding sense of mortality to linger with me. But here was an answer. And really, in some ways, it was the same as my father's.

9

GROWING UP

It was in adolescence that I first began to consider and to question my father's beliefs. I began to think about the Brethren and to wonder why he felt that his only spiritual home was among them. I felt it would have been so much happier, easier, if like other families, we had all gone together to the Parish Church. There would then never have been the rifts and tensions between those who could accept 'the Meeting', and remain loyal to my father, and those who, on their conscience, could not; for my older step-sisters felt passionately on this issue. But my father in his quiet way, remained adamant that this was the right, the Scriptural method by which 'believers' should meet together as a church. He held firmly to the doctrine of 'the priesthood of all believers', based on the teaching of the Bible, which belief he maintained was ignored by the established church where only the ministry of ordained men was normally allowed. Most young people nowadays would find it most boring and tedious to hear long discussions about these subjects. They would not be able to imagine the vehemence of the arguments. But often they went on over my head at the meal table, endlessly to and fro, and for every question there was an answer ready, backed by Scripture.

I knew the Brethren were very unpopular,—and also misunderstood. This was probably because they held that all the main sects had departed from the simple New Testament pattern of worship, organisation and doctrine. In most churches, they claimed, this was now overlaid by many and

76

various traditions of men. Even then, young as I was, I wondered whether all this really mattered. Searching for an answer in a confused way, almost battered and sometimes distressed by the arguments from those who opposed my father, I came alone to a simple uncluttered child-like belief that I must look for the true, the real spirit of Christ in men. Nothing else mattered.

I saw it in my father, in his essentially simple dedicated life. His doctrinal beliefs were not significant to me. It was the man himself I watched. Indeed, in spite of his beliefs he had friends in every sect and denomination, unlike many Plymouth Brethren at that time, and he was loved by his many patients. He never forced his faith on them, or spoke of it unless he was asked to do so. One of his close friends was a Roman Catholic doctor. These two used to talk together with love and freedom of the things in their faith which they held in common. When this doctor lay dying it was my father for whom he asked, it was my father whose hand he held, and who, at his request, read the 23rd Psalm to him as he was passing.

The Brethrens' unpopularity caused an amusing and embarrassing situation on one occasion. I remember a cleric from an Anglican missionary society was dining at our house before some big meeting in the city. We entertained an endless stream of deputation speakers of every variety, size and mentality. During the meal he became expansive.

'I can get on with Christians from every denomination except one,' he held forth. My father started to smile, suspecting what was coming.

'And which is that?' he asked.

'The Plymouth Brethren. I find them impossible.' Our visitor smiled jovially at the listeners he was finding so sympathetic. My father leaned forward.

'Dear me, I am afraid you cannot be enjoying your

dinner,' he said mischievously. A look of surprise came over the missionary's face.

'You are dining with one now', went on my father relentlessly.

'Well, I just can't believe it', said the man, now in consternation. 'You're not like any I've ever met before!'

What was the reason for this guest's attitude? What sort of lives did the Plymouth Brethren lead? I used to think about this.

While many of the adventurous among them travelled over the world as missionaries, often pioneers, fearless where they believed they were led to take the gospel, yet the majority at home were undoubtedly quietists. Many lived very withdrawn lives within a small social group. Because of their seclusion, their love for each other in the family was deep and channelled, and did not obviously flow out to ordinary humanity in the world around them. I had seen many married couples sitting at some small gathering holding hands affectionately, the husband and wife closely dependant on each other. Indeed in some ways families lived a life not dissimilar to that found in a devout Jewish family. The father was indeed a *Paterfamilas*, controller and lawgiver. His was the ultimate decision in any matter. To disobey him would have brought sincere grief to both parents, and a dreadful rift, which could not easily be healed, because one's wrongdoing would be held to be deliberate, and a betrayal of his love.

As in a Jewish family there was the same tight family solidarity, with its care of one member for another. There was real sorrow if a member of the family married 'out'—as is the Jewish phraseology. To marry a Roman Catholic might even mean to cut oneself off from its fellowship for ever. Over and above everything was the enfolding love of a family within which one was almost held in a stranglehold. To break it meant desolation and loneliness. To keep within it could mean imprisonment. Outside of it one belonged nowhere, one just did *not* fit in. Considered odd and eccentric by society, even hypocritical, although this was unjust, the members of the Brethren drew together as small minority groups do, seeking their pleasures and social intercourse only within the safe framework. Various behaviour patterns were consistently seen.

Husband and wife were never heard to argue in public. The wife was the 'helpmeet', and often very much in the background. Never allowed to speak at a meeting, not even the weekly Bible reading or prayer meeting, the women showed a gentle acquiescence which never ceased to astonish me. Their attitude appeared completely sincere. It certainly gives one pause for thought in these days of broken homes, ruined marriages, and desolate children. I met many mother-ly loving women, their interests—entirely unselfish—centred on their husband and family, their simple faith sweet and wholesome. Often I felt irritated by their apparent sub-servience; I was ready to fight their battles. This caused them amusement; they were gently affectionate towards me, the rebel, but they had no battles to fight.

I had to admit that as far as I could see, although the husband was often a little autocratic, he normally showed concern and care and deep affection for his wife. One man I knew, would not consider letting his wife go through a major operation unless he was literally at her side throughout it, and this had to be allowed. He maintained they had never been separated, and he did not intend to be parted from her in this. Indeed in all the husband-wife relationships I saw, there was a strong impression of mutual love and respect. How successful were they in bringing up their families? Here generalisation is not possible. I often saw the love of parents for children apparently happily reproduced, the children appearing to grow up quite contented within the

confines of their parents' belief. On the other hand I knew
more than one family in which at least one child rebelled
at the strict control, and eventually left the shelter of home to
follow his or her own path, without the parents' approval.
In these cases the strain on both sides was very great.

There were certain rules that had to be obeyed, mainly
based on orthodox Christianity, but retaining a great deal of
the Old Testament attitudes, supremely governed by the Law
but also manifested in a number of smaller ways. I remember
on one occasion staying in Cumberland and being given
black pudding to eat, which I found quite appetising. When
I asked for this at home, my father almost lost control. This
was the forbidden thing, the eating of blood, and never never
to be touched again under any circumstance whatsoever. I
was dismayed and astonished at this violent reaction. It put
me off black pudding for life.

Their attitude to public life was generally negative. As a
rule, at that time, they took no part in politics or local government. In this, I felt, they were greatly mistaken. But in day
to day conduct we learned something of great value. Absolute honesty and integrity were demanded in everything we
did, even in the most insignificant detail. Work had never to
deviate from the best. For this reason many of the Brethren
were notable in their vocations or trades, and were greatly
trusted by those who could never have subscribed to their
beliefs and way of life.

The Plymouth Brethren were quite strong numerically in
our city, and mercifully for me I had at least one friend at
school who shared an almost identical background. In-
terestingly enough this produced in her strength of character
and a brilliant arrow-like brain; she won a major scholarship to Cambridge. We both had a great sense of humour and
an ability to comment freely on our state, which carried me
through a lot that otherwise might have been hard to bear.

Like mine, her life was hedged about by the rules. These were enforced in love and were, therefore, almost impossible to break. We were never allowed to visit a theatre or cinema because we were told that here vice and immorality were often portrayed. Moreover, the lives of actors and actresses were notable for moral weakness. My father was reinforced in this view, because one of his cousins had broken away from parental tradition and had gone on the stage, becoming a successful actor. However, his private life ended in a divorce from his beautiful actress wife and in financial ruin. These two things were almost unforgiveable in those days and really caused my father sorrow. I was fascinated to go and watch this cousin in a famous film after I left home. I liked him immensely.

When I was about fifteen, the whole of my form arranged to take the English mistress to the theatre. She was preparing us for examinations and I was fond of her. My father could not bring himself to let me go. I was the only one left out of this celebration. Walking to school that morning, a well-meaning friend asked why I was not going. Briefly I replied, but she knew the truth, and her warm heart was full of sympathy.

'Well, it's a damn shame. That's all I can say', she said.

I think this was the only time that I was utterly demoralised, and could hardly go on to school, because I was crying so bitterly. I was not only crying in self pity. Surprisingly, I was crying because my father, whom I loved, was thought cruel, and I knew he was not. This was a matter of conscience to him. My bitter disappointment had turned me into a traitor to him. I was crying because that day I just could not 'take' his rules, and that was a deep disloyalty I thought. And I could not bear that he should be diminished in the thought of others.

In matters of love and sex, modesty was an absolute 'must',

flirting was forbidden, and one was encouraged to look forward to a career. Marriage might well not be ordained for
one. Sometimes I was on the edge of outright rebellion. Yet
inwardly and secretly I conceded that only the real thing
would do for me. I did not want to hurt or deceive anyone,
but I most certainly wanted fun. It was incomprehensible to
my father that anyone could doubt his rightness in matters of
conduct. Things were so simple to him, black or white, right
or wrong. No problems arose.

As I thought about the little community I knew so well,
certain characteristics were outstanding in my mind. Their
quiet dress, their quiet speech, their real affection for each
other. The women often embraced with a sort of love and
sympathy for each other's welfare. I almost never saw any
of the cliques, the jockeying for position, the jealousies and
envyings which I found later were all too frequent in many
secular bodies and some church groups. Perhaps this was
because it was an imperative laid on every member of the
Brethren to be a living witness to the faith, in every detail of
public and private life. They certainly did not have 'fun',
as the world would understand it. But there was a sort
of innocent glee, an almost childlike enjoyment of the
smallest and simplest pleasures. Their palates were not
jaded. They gazed out on life in daily expectation of
blessings to come, and their expressions were open, clear
and unafraid.

.   .   .   .   .

So the years passed in this quiet setting. Now I reached the
age of seventeen, and felt an intense eagerness to live life to
the full. I worked hard for the Scholarship Entrance Examination to London University, making up for years of a fairly
easy-going attitude to work. I won a place, not a scholarship, in one of the Womens' Colleges, in the English honours

School. It was not my mother's standard. Still, it would do to be going on with. The future was rosy.

Then I began to feel oddly lethargic. I lost interest in everything, and I had a sort of dull pain in my right side. A month before, my half sister, now married to a Professor of Chemistry in London University, had nearly died in a London hospital of a neglected appendix; she had been ill with peritonitis for a long time. Her husband and my father had been very anxious. She was saved by one of London's leading surgeons. Surely I could not be afflicted in the same way? I was busy at school at this time, for as House Captain I was supposed to be organising a great festive end of term tea, and arranging all the catering. I dragged myself around the school feeling sick and ill—and in dread of what was wrong. I collapsed in the sick room with a slight temperature, but eventually was allowed to walk home. Slowly I walked up to the front door. The parlourmaid opened it.

'Where's my father?'

'Out to tea with your mother.' I was sure now it was probably a matter of hours or minutes only until I would be past help. I lay down on a chair, feeling unreal. The present drifted away. At last my parents came in.

'I'm sure I've got appendicitis', I said.

'Impossible', answered my father briskly. However he examined me carefully.

'We'll call Leonard', he said briefly. This was the city's senior surgeon, and a friend and colleague of my father. They did much work together. He appeared almost at once.

'Got the gripes?' he said cheerfully. I nodded. He examined me with careful cool prodding hands. It took a long time.

'Sub-acute appendix. When do you go to college?'

'October.'

'Better without this.' He was cheerful and monosyllabic.

'See you to-morrow, nine thirty.' He departed with a quick wave of the hand.

All my childhood fears returned. I might be in danger of death. I was not ready to die. I had achieved nothing. I tossed and turned. What would my parents do? Surely they could not do without me? I slept fitfully, with nightmare.

In the morning it was the same. I wanted life, to feel the sun on my face, the fresh wind off the sea, to run and leap with the boundless energy inside me, even to cry, but not to finish my life before it had begun. So my thoughts raced to and fro. Full of adolescent emotions I felt on the edge of a precipice.

My father was to take me in his car to the hospital. It was a hot brilliant July day, the sun already beating down on the broad tree-lined streets, the shadows of the leaves falling across the pavements. My father looked gently towards me.

'There's no need for you to be afraid, Anne', he said quietly. My fears must have rushed into my face, and he added, 'In my prayers this morning I had the assurance that you will come through this operation perfectly safely.'

An incredulous hope flooded through me. The sun seemed to shine more brilliantly. So he knew. I turned gratefully, thankfully, to him. I was ashamed. When things went wrong I was like Mr. Faintheart in Bunyan's *Pilgrim's Progress*, swamped with fears and anxieties. One day I must really grow up, stand on my own feet, find my own way to God, be prepared to stand alone. But now, surely, God had sent my father to speak to me.

I walked quite composedly into the hospital.

.   .   .   .   .

The day came at last when I was going to leave home, to go to the University. My trunk was strapped waiting in the hall, and suffocated with excitement I could hardly wait for the taxi to come. The door to freedom was gently opening, and my heart and mind were in a ferment. The taxi arrived. It smelt of leather and old boots.

We reached the station. The express train with its mighty engine, slid alongside the platform, steam pouring and hissing out of the funnel. I climbed into the third class carriage, and stood at the train window. My mother looked sad. My father had vanished. Where had he gone? Soon he came back, almost running. He was passionately interested in trains.

'I say, I've been in the engine cab, it's a 4-6-0 engine, the King George Vth.—Wonderful train.' It was the face of an eager school boy. The train started to move. His face saddened, suddenly desolate. I could not say anything. What would he do without me to make him laugh?

'Goodbye, darling. God bless you.' Suddenly I knew he needed me, even as all these years I had relied on him.

'Goodbye, now. I'll write.'

Doors slammed, the whistle blew. Slowly the train gathered speed, gliding round the curved track, heading eastwards.

A surging hope rose in me. I was going out to meet the future. I wanted to experience everything. I was ready for living, for loving. I would never wholly leave him, and I hoped he would understand if mine was a different path. My own life was beginning.

I turned my face towards London.

G

IO

UNDERGRADUATE

THE bright new morning when I set out for the University found me with enough optimism for ten people, and a great hopefulness. It was at that moment that I first left my father and began gropingly to make a life of my own.

I sat in the railway carriage that was heading smoothly towards London, thinking over the last few weeks. First I thought about my mother. It had been quite hard for her to find enough money to get all the things I needed, crockery, cutlery, clothes, a large trunk. In fact, those clothes that were not bought carefully at the less expensive shops, were home made. My mother was skilled at dressmaking and had contrived to create two or three evening dresses for me, necessary for formal college dining. She had seemed as excited as I was, talking over her own college days as the sewing machine whirred busily, and she swiftly cut out, pinned and tacked. Sometimes she held a row of pins firmly between her teeth, and I used to cry out, 'Don't do it, You'll swallow them—I'm sure you will', and she would be very slow to take them out, just to tease me. Now she was sad I knew, in spite of all her talk, because the house would be quiet and lonely when I was gone. My father was out seeing his patients for long hours and, although she did much public work, my mother was reticent and shy and told no one much about her own troubles, although people would pour out their confidences to her and she was always ready to help anyone. She had become graver, more pre-occupied over the years. She seemed intent I thought, to try and live up to my father's standards; her life was quiet, uneventful, and her main outlet was her varied educational work for the schools in the city.

Hitherto my father had dominated my life, gently, inexorably, but the reins were held tight. Now, in a way, I was entering my mother's world, and whatever I had in me of her character and mood came uppermost.

It was not from her, however, that there came into my mind a kind of rejection of the form of worship my father followed. I would forget the Plymouth Brethren at college, I would never mention them. It was all too different, too demanding, and I longed for beauty and music in religion. I *must* be the same as other people, for I thought no one would understand my home, and this I found intolerable. I had longed to fill the large dignified house with gaiety and fun and parties, and the quietness and restraint had sometimes been terrible to me. Also I did not want anyone to think I was odd, in any way. Most of all I felt a loneliness. Would I ever find friends I could tell about my home? I thought this was unlikely; and until I could be accepted with this background which seemed to me so unusual I knew I could give my whole confidence to none.

With thoughts like these racing through my mind, I left the London train at Reading and changed to a slower moving train which wound through the lovely countryside of Berkshire and Surrey, splashed with the brilliant reds and golds of autumn. At Egham Station, I lifted my suitcase off the rack, breathed deeply the brisk early October air, climbed down onto the platform and got into a taxi.

Swiftly it mounted the long steep hill, and before me at the top lay the great ornamented gates, and the almost incredible red and white brick vastness of the Royal Holloway College for Women, part of the University of London. Its many domes, towers, pinnacles and pseudo-Gothic architecture proclaimed it a copy—as it was—of the French chateau of Chambôrd, but the college was on a vaster and more massive scale. Its many corridors were an eighth of a mile long and one could barely see from one end of them to the other.

Imposing, impossible edifice as it was, it never prevented me from feeling somehow 'at home' in it, from the moment I stepped out of the taxi; and entering a hall on East ground floor, as the bottom corridor was called, I presented myself at the little window of an office. A bespectacled face with somewhat unnatural black hair, topped by a starched white cap, peered out at me. This was the formidable figure of Portress who, I was to learn, watched over our goings out and comings in. I was told the number of my rooms. They were on East one, the corridor immediately above, and up two broad imposing flights of stone stairs.

Like every other student I had a small study and bedroom, sparsely but adequately furnished. My study window looked out on lawns and stone balustrades, broad paths and stone steps to lower grounds where trees and meadows stretched into the distance. The bedroom immediately opposite the study looked inwards into the Queen's 'Quad'. In the centre of this great quadrangle, Queen Victoria, in widow's weeds, stood expressionless by a solid armchair, in white smooth stone, appearing to show faint disapproval at the emancipation of women. In the centre of the adjoining Founder's 'Quad', stood another figure immortalised in stone. Tall and dignified, of noble expression, Thomas Holloway, patent pill manufacturer, stood clasping a scroll and gazing at us for ever with benign approbation, donor of this monumental pile given to the world for the higher education of women. He had made his money by manufacturing patent medicines and he was a sort of Nuffield of his day, giving away much of his great fortune to various mammoth enterprises of a charitable nature for the good of mankind.

That first afternoon I remember meeting about six 'Freshers' like myself, all feeling strange and new, and we made tea together in one of the studies. A feeling of freedom began to seize me. As the days passed, friendships were quickly made. I felt I loved the whole world, I could imagine no better life. Even the getting up each day, on those cool autumn mornings when the scent of coffee hung heavy in the corridors which lay near the great dining-hall, was to awake to happiness. I would listen intently in the ten minutes of compulsory college chapel each morning, to see if I could come to any conclusion about my own faith. But after it was over, solemnity was forgotten, we would fling off our 'gowns' and mortar boards, which most of us wore at a jaunty angle, and rush to secure places at breakfast.

On the first Sunday evening all first year students gathered in the lofty and imposing picture gallery for a formidable event known as 'Slave Market'. This ordeal meant that one waited for those superior beings, second and third year students, to ask one to be a dinner partner one night in the term if they so wished, and thereafter we had to choose our own dinner partners from among our own year. Evening dinner was an event of great formality. All students in the college gathered in evening or semi-evening dress each night, just before seven o'clock in the long library, to await the Principal's procession of Dons and guests which left her rooms two by two. They would sweep through the library and picture gallery, out into the corridor, and eventually into the vast dining hall and to the High Table. The two butlers and many maids stood waiting along the hall to serve the dinner. One sat near or far from 'High' according to rank and seniority.

Everyone joined behind the Principal's procession with the partner of the evening, third year students leading, headed by the Senior Student of the year, a godlike figure to me then. First year students, a little unsure at first and selfconscious, brought up the rear. The Principal, the great and formidable Miss Higgins, beloved, however, to generations of students, sat, imposing in a black satin evening gown, decorated with gold braid, at the centre of the High table. Her hair was cut in a loose 'Eton crop', short like a man's. The strong unusual face, stern and commanding in repose, could flash from time to time into a humorous smile and the apparent fierceness melt into understanding and sympathy.

On many nights she had a student partner, for it was her policy to get to know us all. However, the formal white card left in the metal holder on one's door which held one's name, struck terror into the heart: 'The Principal requests the pleasure of your company to dine with her at the High Table tonight.' I believe that if one survived easily this ordeal, no social engagement in later life could deter or undermine one. Those not gifted at easy talk would be put under a dreadful strain, as she left her partner to start the conversation. If nothing was forthcoming, her expression lapsed into brooding sternness. A gay and spontaneous student delighted her and she would throw back her head laughing heartily at any amusing anecdote.

Some students had come from homes where this etiquette and formality were inconceivable. I was fortunate, perhaps, because although I looked out on life with naiveté and a sort of innocence then, I was at least used to social manners, and I received many invitations to be a dinner partner from those senior to me. During these evenings I got to know and be friendly with people of great character and versatility. Conversation had always been a pleasure to me, but often it was carefree chatter. Now I had to match my wits with a number of sparkling intellects. Laughter was nearly always present. An entirely serious dinner was unusual.

In this 'set-up', I remember, there were those who could not fit in. A little student from Devonshire found no compatible friends. She had obviously been the heroine of a poor family who had found it a great financial strain to send her to college. She was a fish out of water, unsophisticated, uneasy in talk, and I remember my pity for her and feelings of inadequacy when she came to me crying bitterly because she was overwhelmed with loneliness. I, who was so happy now, had so little to give her. I found her a strain to be with; and yet she was as honest as the day, and I could imagine her in her own setting among the little hills and fields, by the rocky coast where her village lay. Here she would be admired for her good brain and would be outstanding among her own homely folk who loved her. Her mother died while she was still at college. Her sorrow overflowed as she worried over her younger brothers and sisters. I realised that for some the University could be a cruel and lonely place.

I became engrossed in the work itself. Studying the great span of English literature I listened, as it were, to other voices from the past. I tried to assess what they found in life, what prompted their emotions, love, sorrow, despair, and religious ecstasy. All these could be found in the medieval and Elizabethan writers. These were my favourite periods. Their spontaneity, simplicity and vigorous acceptance of life were qualities I admired. Also, they had a happiness and rollicking *joie-de-vivre* with which I felt far more at home than with some of the much more mannered eighteenth and early nineteenth century literature.

Outside of work, my first reaction was to absorb as much gaiety and friendship as I could. I joined everything, and first the College Dramatic Society, which each year put on really notable productions. In doing this I broke firmly from Puritan tradition and, when I took a leading part in

Congreve's play, *The Way of the World*, I hardly felt the same person. I played hockey and, on getting into the 1st XI, found I could spend many Saturdays in and around London, playing against other colleges; all our travelling expenses were paid. We would end the day with a cheap but exotic meal in the brasserie of a Lyon's Corner House, often accompanied by the music of a Swiss or Austrian orchestra. Then we would queue to sit in 'the gods'—the balcony of the Old Vic, or Sadler's Wells. This cost sixpence. Neck craning forward, I would gaze through the shimmering beam of the spotlights, lost in the thrill of the best dramatic performances of the day. I remember a young John Gielgud as Hamlet, violently destroyed by his own character; and Dame Edith Evans as Rosalind in *As You Like It*, enchanting in her gaiety and delicacy of movement.

We would take the last bus back to college. Even standing on the cold pavement in a blustery wind as midnight was approaching in London, was happiness. As the stars came out, the deep booming voice of Big Ben would reverberate across the city. Late night revellers, top hats tilted on the backs of their heads, white silk scarves wound carelessly round the neck, would saunter by, with their girls. Or, sometimes, a tramp would be seen shuffling along, combing the gutters for cigarette stubs. There was the ceaseless roar of traffic that to me was a lovely sound speaking of journeys and wanderings; at this hour it would begin to lessen, and we would swing onto the bus, often accompanied by a few drunks, or others like ourselves who had been to late shows, and so we would pass quickly through the sleeping suburbs, where the lights were going out, one by one.

Just after midnight, the vast ornamented silhouette of the college would appear, massive, impervious, on top of the hill, and we would climb out and creep quickly into college . . . and there was always tomorrow.

Each day had its own happiness. Life was radiant and one could hardly savour it enough.

Close friendships were inevitable in a women's college and on the whole were normal, although I knew of some which became altogether too intense. Usually we would talk endlessly and far into the night, drinking many cups of coffee, the air thick with cigarette smoke. There was a saying then, 'First years sit up late and talk about their souls; second years sit up late and talk about themselves; third years go to bed early.' On the whole, I avoided the subject of the soul. I was more interested in personalities. I suppose we were not much different from our modern counterparts, except in one particular. There was far less of the free and easy companionship between men and women students. Occasionally we went to University dances in London, but, on the whole, we were rather secluded and a little cut off. I am surprised now to recollect how little sense of deprivation I felt. But in a way life was absorbing in its own right, and I felt I must enjoy whatever it offered at that particular moment. Indeed I was in no hurry to rush past this stage.

So it was that, for the moment, I enjoyed life and tried to forget the future. In any case, I viewed certain escapades of my friends with some amusement and perhaps a little cynicism, and in one case, with some pity. One of the girls on my corridor was having a rather long and tedious association with a dull-looking man—or so I thought him. She was carefree and goodnatured, and her attitude to men was expansive and optimistic. 'Easy come, easy go,' was her way and she was for ever hoping for her ideal. One evening she went out with this same Charles—he had been a faithful attendant for a long time—and it being summer, they found a convenient field with high hedges and sat down. A farmer was out with his gun, on the other side of the hedge and, hearing their movements, he mistook them for rabbits and shot at them. Jane was wounded in the forehead but poor Charles was shot in the face and eye. They staggered out, bleeding profusely, to get help, and a passing car rushed them to Windsor Hospital. Poor Charles lost an eye and Jane carried a T-shaped scar on her brow for life, thereafter. It seemed rather a melodramatic waste, I thought, for one evening's brief pleasure.

Although some of my friends had various boys they were fond of, most of them were quite firm at this time in wanting a career before marriage. Only one, I remember, was entirely carefree about life. She was wealthy, had a sports car, and failed her examinations regularly. 'I'll just stay here until my hockey boots are worn out,' she would say—and she did. I think that most of us wanted, in a way, to prove ourselves. Moreover, between 1935 and 1938, the threat of war was getting more and more ominous. It was clear that our future was precarious.

But yet we were happy. After an especially hard spell of work, we would gather for a party in someone's room. One of these proved a little unusual. A certain student, a rather colourful personality, and one of the very few of the wealthy among us, was to come to one of these hilarious evenings. She was quite a wit and told fantastic, but I believe entirely true, stories of her early life. Her father was—remarkably—over eighty when she was born, and she told how he used to push her in her pram when she was a baby. She had a fund of improbable anecdotes to relate, but among them she told us she was psychic. This we did not then believe, although she was sincere enough. So we said we would put it to the test. We decided, in agnostic mood, to hold an experiment. In the small room, eight of us including Dorothy, gathered round a three foot square table, hands placed next to each other, flat on the table top, little fingers touching. We were about to try 'table-turning' and were sworn to play fair. The evening, which started in high spirits, ended soberly. After a very long silence, a tremor passed through Dorothy, she became glassy-eyed and almost unconscious, and went into a trance. The table started to move, at first jerkily then steadily towards the door, and then out of the door. Our hands lay lightly on it, exerting no pressure, and we moved rigidly and clumsily alongside it. Dorothy then nearly fainted, and the table paused in its career. We were a little subdued, as this was odd and inexplicable, and we vaguely, perhaps uneasily, put it down to 'animal magnetism'. Dorothy felt ill for the rest of the evening and we all wondered.

Life at college often held interesting and humorous episodes. The college's jubilee celebrations provided a memorable day. Queen Mary was to come and visit us on this auspicious occasion, accompanied by the charming Princess Alice, Countess of Athlone. Various ceremonies including a concert, the planting of a tree, and a service in chapel, were arranged, and we were all carefully coached in our curtseys and general demeanour. I was one of the choir of some thirty people who were to sing to the Queen. Although the standard of music was already high, we had never rehearsed so ardently.

Some twenty minutes or more before the Queen was due, while the students were moving through the building to their allotted places, one of the academic staff asked me to run swiftly to the north tower—which was situated at the main entrance of the college itself—with a message. Clad, as by instruction, in best clothes shrouded in a black undergraduate's gown, and—not by instruction—with mortar board hastily clapped at a cock-eyed angle on one side of the head, I swiftly took to my heels so that I might be back in my place in time to await the arrival of the Royal party. Emerging at high speed from a long corridor, which led out into the open cloister approaching the Tower, I found I was running fast and headlong into an imposing procession. Horrified, I realised I was wedged irrevocably between the door behind and Queen Mary in front, who, like a splendid galleon in full sail, was relentlessly bearing down upon me, accompanied by Princess Alice, the Principal and a bevy of governors. It was difficult to brake. At very serious risk of fracturing a leg, I flung myself into a sort of contorted curtsey as, at the same time, I tried to back hastily off the path onto a flower bed. My strange acrobatics were graciously acknowledged with a brief nod and a quizzical look. Why had no one warned us that the Queen was always early?

As the group swept into the corridor I delivered the message and slunk back to my appointed place, where my friends, waiting to greet the Queen, were rocking with laughter. Gazing out of a window they had observed the whole scene.

'What on *earth* were you doing literally *prostrating* yourself on the path at the feet of the Queen?' asked one. I was mortified.

Later Queen Mary took tea at the High Table in hall. It happened that my seat was at the end of one of the long tables by which she passed when the meal was over. Again, but this time very correctly, I curtsied when she drew level with me. Suddenly, she almost paused, gazed at me with penetrating, faintly amused, very blue eyes, and the dignified beautiful face relaxed into a warm smile. In imagination I could almost hear her say in her remarkable deep melodious voice, 'What! you again!'

By the time she had listened to the concert, and had asked for one song, *Music, when soft voices die*, to be repeated for her especial pleasure—almost a sad pleasure, I thought—I had come completely under the influence of her grave charm.

I enjoyed every side of college life. I still pondered very deeply on the Christian faith. I was made Social Secretary of the Student Christian movement, where the various branches of social work in which we took part were most rewarding.

A few of my friends held firm and deep religious beliefs, and Christianity was often argued and discussed. At this time I told almost no one about my home background. But I found it stimulating to be in an atmosphere where one could be agnostic or atheist freely; and this was because, for the first time in my life, my own weak, unsure, and wavering faith was strengthened by opposition—for I could believe in something I had to fight for; whereas at home it had been nearly extinguished by my father's overpowering Christian belief which brooked no doubts or questionings because to him it was life itself.

II

'IN SIMPLE TRUST'

LIFE at college passed smoothly and happily at first. We were in a small world of learning, of exploration in thought and ideas. Sometimes it was a quiet world where one could retreat into one of the many book-lined recesses of the great college library, light a green-shaded lamp on the table, which cast a vivid glow on one's books and papers, and become deeply involved in unravelling and solving the deeper problems and meanings in literary texts.

But outside in the world the years were stormy. They had seemed happy enough. One brilliant evening of early summer, the sky still blue and light, we took, as we often did, a punt out on the Thames. It was hot and close, and the long shafts of golden light across the sky were like a farewell before the night and, indeed, in one way an epoch was coming to an end.

The Thames was like fairyland as we punted east towards London. Every garden sloping to the water was decorated with flags and flowery arches and everywhere along the banks people were singing or standing and laughing together and everyone was waiting for the hour to strike.

Suddenly, as the sky dimmed into dusk, a million fairy lights were turned on, myriads of colours, flashing and twinkling. Streams of gold, silver, blue, red and green merged and trembled, reflected across the gently moving water. It was unbelievably beautiful.

We drew our punt to the side and joined a party of people who had just switched on a radio in their garden. Harsh, but full of emotion, the voice of King George V echoed clearly across the river as he spoke to his 'beloved people', for this was his Silver Jubilee. London had gone wild that day in demonstrations of loyalty as the old King and Queen Mary drove through the streets, and he was deeply moved. Now everyone felt drawn together, perhaps in a confused love of country and affection for a simple man. Here on the Thames, at the heart of England, the scene was caught and held forever in the mind.

Not many months passed before the King died and the violent upheaval of the abdication and the crowning of another king took place.

On the night of the Coronation of George VI, a friend and I took a train to Victoria and, on foot, fought our way through the vast crowds and, somehow, struggling and pushing, tried to reach the front of Buckingham Palace. Famous people jostled and thrust through the vast good-natured crowds. We came face-to-face with Lord Baden-Powell in Scout uniform and then were carried forward in a surging mass, all singing and shouting, 'For he's a jolly good fellow' and 'We want the King.' We had somehow arrived at the gates of the Palace.

Suddenly, the tall central windows were opened and the young King and Queen, dazzling in dress, radiant in appearance, hiding for this night whatever doubts and fears beset them, appeared on the balcony. Such a roar of acclamation went up, it seemed the heavens might crack. Then a sudden silence fell, and quite spontaneously the crowd started to sing the National Anthem. Everyone was friends with his neighbour, the crowd was jubilant, swept along on a great tide of happiness.

My final year began. There was uneasiness in the world, we were approaching the abyss. At home, a terrible poverty had fallen on the North East of England, a district that was strangely in my mind at that time. The hunger-marchers came from Jarrow to London. There was no work for an honest man. The shipyards were idle. Outside the country, events were moving swiftly. Mussolini had used mustard gas in his unprovoked attack on the country of Ethiopia, whose noble Emperor, tiny in stature, great in heart, called in vain for help. How could I dream, then, that in a few brief years my parents would be having tea with him, quietly in my own city of Bath? For he was to become, like so many, an exile. Hitler shouted and threatened, and there was everywhere, it seemed, the sound of marching. Life became unsure, and a chill foreboding seized the minds of my generation.

Then my own life changed overnight. Perhaps quite suddenly I grew up. I was due to take my final examinations in June and was well aware that I must keep up an all-out effort. I worked long hours, often before breakfast and sometimes far into the night. Money was short at home. I knew I must start to earn my own living immediately I had qualified.

One day in February I was going into lunch when the college Bursar came up to me, grave and looking concerned.

'I have some disturbing news for you', she said. 'Your father has had a stroke and you must go home for a night or two.'

A coldness came over me. No, it was impossible. Thin people with endless vitality did not get strokes. He was too alive, too full of dynamic energy. It must be a mistake, or . . . was this just a preparation for worse.

'Is he alive?' My voice was hard. I was crying in my mind but was unable to sound anything but cold.

'Oh yes, he is alive; but I think you should have a quick lunch and get home as soon as possible.' One of my friends came up.

'Dad's had a stroke', I said unbelievingly.

Any way, no-one knew what I felt about him, and I was

not going to tell anyone now. It was all unreal and I felt as if this must be happening in a play. My friend stayed with me while I put a few clothes in a suitcase, she ordered a taxi, saw me off, gripping my hand before I went. Her own father had died the year before and she sensed my feelings, I think.

The journey was endless. I felt sick. How could God let him have a stroke which would make him helpless? He had done nothing but help people all his life, he had never spared himself.

At last I reached home. The parlourmaid opened the door, looking anxious.

'What's happened, Gladys?' The words would hardly come.

'Your father is very ill', she said, obviously upset. My mother suddenly appeared beside me, trying to look calm and easy—for my sake I knew.

'Darling, how good of you to come.'

'What's happened?' My voice did not seem right.

My mother led me upstairs, talking calmly, but her face belied her.

'Dr. Sutherland says it's a stroke. It all happened because poor Mrs. Buchanan is dying. Her doctor refused to go and see her at night—what a cruel thing!—they rang Daddy and, of course, although he had gone to bed he just leapt up and dashed straight out. He was out two hours or more and, when he came home, he ran upstairs—you know how he does', her voice was unsteady, 'and as he came into the room he fell unconscious on the floor. I just could not get him lifted into bed. It was terrible. But Dr. Sutherland came in five minutes. He has been wonderful, and saved his life I think.'

'I'll go in now', my hand was on the door handle, but I paused. I felt I could not see him like this. He had been to so many like a rock in a weary land—wasn't that what the old

H

hymn said? The words ridiculously came back and echoed to and fro in my head. I imagined a negro singing, as in *Uncle Tom's Cabin*, swaying to and fro, 'Oh! Jesus is a rock in a weary land, in a weary land, in a weary land.' He had so often been my rock and I felt I had seen God in him.

At last I went towards the bed and saw the quiet, motionless figure, not even aware I was there. I knew, then, he might die. Drained of life and vitality and emotion, the face still showed traces of nobility and steadfastness. I felt that, perhaps now, I had really lost him. I could ignore him, rebel against him, but now I was drawn back to him in grief, and I knew then it would always be so.

'Dad, I've come.' I took his hand, almost lifeless it seemed. Miraculously, a tiny tremor seemed to pass from him to me, there was the faintest movement, the eyelids lifted a fraction, and the ghost, the echo of a smile came and went.

I stayed at home three days. I learned we had almost no money in the bank. Things had been hard for a long time. Patients were slow to pay their bills and the new bills had not gone out yet. Our doctor had told my mother that everything must be sold up immediately, our lovely house, the practice, the car. We had almost nothing to live on until the proceeds of this sale came in, if, indeed, any sale could be negotiated at this time. My mother was obviously deeply worried and I felt uneasy at leaving her. My father had improved, hardly perceptibly, but he was still alive, and that morning he murmured two or three words to me. They were very sad. He tried to raise his hand. It was impossible. He had strong, well-shaped hands, skilled and gentle when examining a patient, never fumbling, always sure and firm.

'I used to be proud of my hands.' It was a sigh almost and the voice died away. He drifted back into sleep or unconsciousness. What torture this must be for him, I thought.

For the first time in my life there was no-one to see me

off at the station. Now I was alone. I must go back to college and work as never before. I must start applying for September jobs at once and I would have to teach. There was no time now to take further training to be a hospital almoner, which I had really wanted. It was work or starve, and what was to happen until September?

The future just then seemed dark. Well—perhaps I must do what my father had taught me. Perhaps in my own inadequate way I must try and take his place . . . but just now there was only one thing I had better do, I would do as he had taught me. I would pray.

The thought of my parents being virtually destitute hung over me. Of course, my father had given away so much of his income to 'the Lord's work' that I had always known he would end up a poor man. I was sometimes irritated by this on my mother's account. Moreover, surely it was time for some heavenly reward to come his way, instead of this rather desperate state of affairs?

I had been back at college about a week when I had a letter from my mother. 'Such a wonderful thing, I can hardly believe it', she wrote. It appeared that the day before, a letter from London had arrived for my father. She opened it and, to her amazement, out fell a cheque for £400. Hardly able to believe what she saw, she read the enclosed letter from their London solicitor. It told her that, many years before, perhaps even before her marriage, my father had been left a share in some London property which had greatly deteriorated and had become virtually a slum. It had been entirely against his principles to own any slum property and he had immediately instructed the solicitor to sell his share. It was typical of him that, having done his duty as he saw it, he should forget the whole matter. In any case, he regarded the property as valueless and really did not expect any financial return. In part he was right—the property was of little

value until now, many years later, it was to be bought up by
the Borough Council, and the cheque was for the sale at
valuation. To my mother this was a wonderful token that
there was One who had not forgotten them and that whatever remained in life they were not alone. For a long time I
thought about this. I really believed, and I do not now deny,
that for those with a profound and simple faith, a remarkable
vindication occurs from time to time of their complete trust
in God. It was not odd, therefore, that this should have
happened to my father.

My memory was saturated with the hymns I had heard
over and over again as a child. Sometimes, they provided a
sort of cant or trivial answer to every question the mind
posed, the lines leaping, unbidden and almost annoyingly
to the mind. But I could not, perhaps unfortunately for me,
easily believe in the easy answer, the evangelical explanation.
Everything must be forged on the anvil of experience, fired,
tested, re-made, before it could be valid. Yet, as I read this
letter, I could hear, in imagination—or was it recollection?—
my father's voice reading a hymn, and the words echoed
through my mind:

'In simple trust like theirs who heard,
    Beside the Syrian sea,
  The gracious calling of the Lord,
  Let us, like them, without a word,
    Rise up and follow thee.'

It seemed to me that Christ literally meant his followers
must become like little children, for only so were they great
enough to be small, small in the presence of the living God,
pure enough to have that 'simple trust'. Well, now I had
seen one answer to a man whose trust had never failed, even
in the darkest hours of his life. I felt inclined to watch for
more. I would need a miracle myself if I was to get a job, for,

unlikely as it seems now, it was hard at that time to get a good teaching post. Some forty people would be applying for many of the jobs advertised and I had not even a Diploma in Education.

Moreover, I now wondered if I was going to pass finals at all. £400 might see us through to September, but I knew it might be a very long time before the practice was sold, and I could have no job without a degree. I became tired and anxious and could not remember all I wanted.

Each morning I got up at about six o'clock and started to send in endless complicated forms applying for teaching posts for the following September. I wrote all over the country, sending letters of application, forms, stamped envelopes, but I had nothing yet to offer any school.

'Please let a miracle happen.' I would send up a prayer as I wrote on and on, alone in the college library, the only warm place at that hour, a grey dawn perhaps just faintly appearing outside. I would sit in a little pool of light from the lamp on the table, while the rest of the great room, with its many alcoves, its book-lined walls rising high above me, would be left in semi-darkness.

I had one interview with a kind but rather fierce headmistress of a girls' High School in the Midlands.

'My dear', she said, 'these testimonials are pleasing, but I need someone with more experience. I hope you will find something suitable.' I had gone up to London to see her, and felt almost instinctively I did not want the job anyway.

I had applied for nearly forty posts and now the early summer was with us. It was a matter of weeks only until Finals. I was downhearted and really concerned. Looking through a list of jobs in the *Times Educational Supplement* one morning, I saw a post advertised in Newcastle upon Tyne. I read it over twice. 'A young mistress would be suitable, willing to train under the Headmistress.' The advertisement stood out, and unbelievably, a voice seemed to reiterate over and over again in my mind, 'That is where you have got to go.'

'But that's too far from home with my father so ill'. I was answering someone or something.

'No. This is your job, and this is where you must go.' The far North, the land of industry and depression and unemployment. I was amazed. Even as I read over the words again, I saw in my mind's eye the great rolling hills of the Border country and a wild wind swept over the moors and I felt in that moment as if I was freed from all that was false in my thinking. I must go North; I believe I will live if I go North, I thought. But here I cannot find a true faith for myself. Perhaps there I will find what I have been looking for so long.

It was a strange experience to feel this compulsion, uncannily, unreasonably strong. I still recollect some of the thoughts and arguments that raced through my mind. I certainly wanted to work where there was a challenge; I often read books on social problems and felt drawn to live where life was tough and real. *Digging with the Unemployed*, was one. *God in the Slums*, was another. Hastily, but carefully, I wrote an application, walked outside to the pillar box at the great gates, and posted it.

Now I am going to ask for my miracle, I thought.

.   .   .   .   .

Each day I waited for the mail, hardly daring to hope for anything except the usual returning of testimonials and the note of regret that the post was now filled.

One morning I had a letter from rather an exclusive independent girls' school in Kent, where daughters of ambassadors and diplomats and members of county families, often sisters of Eton boys, were educated. The headmistress asked me to go down for an interview the following Saturday, and the courteous letter said that she was very interested in my application. The salary was Burnham scale—the best one could get—and there was excellent accommodation for staff outside the school and very few out-of-school duties.

Things were still critical at home. My father was, incredibly, improving very slowly, but was still bedridden, and the practice had not yet been sold, although one or two doctors had shown a faint interest. But money was scarce for many people. It was a very bad time for selling anything.

The new college Principal knew all this, and had been unusually kind to me the last few months and had asked me to talk over any possible jobs with her. I took the letter to show her. She was delighted, and said, 'If you get the chance of this post, snatch at it. It would be ideal for you and not too far from home.' I hardly knew how to tell her about my other application. I hesitated.

'I have applied for a job in the North that I'm rather interested in', I said. 'It's a grant-aided girls' grammar school, a Church foundation, and it's in the area where the "depression" is affecting everything . . .' My voice petered out.

The principal leaned forward and peered at me. 'My dear girl . . .' She obviously thought I was unbalanced. 'Have you ever heard from the Head about your application?'

'No.'

'Well, forget it and do all you can to get this suitable job. You know well that good posts are almost impossible to get without a teaching diploma as well as a degree. Let me know the result of this interview.'

A great depression seized me as I left her study. Obviously I was going to get no more help or advice, at least not the advice I wanted. Although I hadn't heard from that job in Newcastle I was sure, sure as anyone can be, that I had to go there. But why? Was I, perhaps, getting queer as Finals approached? Some people did, but my friends and I were cheerful on the whole, although I knew I was flagging because of all the extra work involved in applying for jobs.

On the morning of my interview in Kent, a letter arrived from the grammar school in the North. The headmistress wished to see me in London the following week. Now what must I do? I knew I might not even get the job. Heads usually interviewed a number of candidates.

Very thoughtfully I set out for a small and picturesque town in Kent, from where wealthy Londoners commuted daily. I walked out of the station and took a short bus journey past many large houses set in beautiful extensive gardens, past tree-lined avenues, and I saw glimpses of the rolling countryside beyond the homes. I came to some very large and imposing gates with two red-tiled cottages near them and a long drive through parkland. The drive curved and there stood a vast mansion with a lofty pillared portico. One of the stateliest of England's stately homes, I thought; not a blade of grass looked out of place on the smooth lawns, the paths were swept and neat, and the whole place gave an air of being wealthy and well cared for.

'Really, it's a palace', I muttered to myself. 'How fearful to live in a palace!' In my mind I felt again the wild, cold wind storming across the moors of Northumberland, where I had never been, and I saw in imagination the smoking chimneys and endless roofs of an industrial town. 'I shall sink into total uselessness if I stay here', I thought, as I gazed at the dignified arched door and pulled a long-handled bell pull.

A maid showed me into a large entrance hall, where I was received with kindness by a sweet-faced middle-aged woman with greying hair. She was obviously a 'gentlewoman' in the old sense—just the sort my aunts would approve of, I thought. 'Do come in, we are so glad to see you. Now, I have tea ready for you first. I am sure you will be glad of it. Then I will show you over the school. Unfortunately, our head-mistress, Miss Brown, is in bed with a sore throat—I am the second mistress—but she will interview you later.'

The trouble is, I thought, after an excellent tea, as I followed this kindly woman from one beautiful room to another, gazing critically at class-rooms and dormitories which all had lovely views from the windows, and eyeing the pleasant daughters of England's privileged people—the only trouble is, there's absolutely nothing wrong with this job, and I'm sure that for some extraordinary reason it's going to be handed to me on a plate.

'We have such a delightful cottage where you can live with three other young members of staff', the gentle voice went on. I was taken round the cottage. It was a little dream house. 'And, of course, except for one night a week, you will be free after school hours.' It was all too good to be true. It was a job any of my friends would have been glad to get. Per-haps, I thought hopefully, I shall not be offered it.

I was taken into the bedroom of the Headmistress, where she lay in a large bed with a gold coverlet. She was a hand-some, rather sophisticated woman. She talked to me for a long time. It appeared this was a most desirable school to work in. Then she smiled suddenly. 'I believe you would be very happy here. I am going to offer you the post', she said. I was completely silenced. A terrible conflict of thoughts chased through my mind. Dear heaven, what was I to do? I took a deep breath.

'I am so grateful you should offer me the post', I said, 'but I feel I must tell you that I have an interview next Saturday for a grammar school in the North of England, and I have a great wish to go to this interview, so I am finding it very difficult to know what to say.' The room was completely still. Now I had burned my boats. I would very likely be rejected for the North job and obviously they would not want me here now when I seemed so uncertain. Visions of my parents destitute came up before me, and I without work. I was crazy, absolutely crazy.

The Head, and I shall always remember her with gratitude, looked at me quizzically. 'You know, if you want to work in that sort of area, this is not the place for you.'

Now panic seized me.

'Yes, I know, but I can't tell until I have had the interview.'

'Yes, I see that. Well . . .' There was a long silence. I could not face my Principal now. I need expect no more help or sympathy. 'Well, it's really rather unprecedented', the Head was speaking, 'but I would like you to come, so I am going to keep this post open for you, provided you let me know your decision immediately after the interview.' It was this thoughtfulness that has kept the memory of that interview vivid until this day. I was saved. I could hardly say 'Thank you' enough.

I saw my Principal that night.

'How did you get on?'

'Well, I got the offer of the job, but the Head is willing to wait a week . . .'

'Wait a week! You know I just cannot understand you. You would be better in this post in every way. You *must* think this over carefully.' I was weighed in the balances, found wanting, and dismissed.

The week dragged on.

The following Saturday, I dressed with great care, put on my one and only best hat—I never wore hats—tilted it just so much, but no more. It matched my best blue suit. I viewed myself in the glass.

'You look fearfully respectable', one friend said, 'You will just suit those Northerners. They're all pretty homely. Though why you want to go and live among the slag heaps I don't know. I couldn't stand it.' I did not know why, either.

I took the bus to central London, went to the offices of the Assistant Mistresses' Association, where candidates for posts at long distances were often interviewed by Heads. I climbed the rather shabby, lino-covered stairs, knocked at the door where I was directed.

A rather tired voice said 'Come in.' I opened the door and a tall, middle-aged woman stood up and shook my hand. I looked at her with a strange sense of destiny. Her clothes were neat but plain; she wore a dark blue felt hat and a navy blue suit. I saw a face slighly lined and careworn, but with a suggestion of humour—somehow it suggested to me a traveller from a land much harder and tougher than my own; but most of all I saw it was one of the most honest and truly good faces I had known. Here was someone in whom, remarkably, with no word spoken, I had implicit trust and, above all, someone for whom I wanted to work.

She talked to me for a long time. After a few questions she spent most of the time telling me in detail the difficulties and frustrations connected with this post. Many of the girls were not up to standard in her opinion. Most had parents who, one way or another, were greatly affected by the depression. The area was hard-hit, lodgings were hard to get, the staff were small in number and overworked, as the timetable was exceedingly heavy. The new buildings were very functional, not at all luxurious.

Eventually, she smiled. 'You won't want to come now if I do offer you the post', she said. It was a question really. Suddenly I felt a great lightness of heart. Why, it was difficulties I wanted. It was a tough assignment I longed for. I had got to prove myself; this was vital to me if ever I was to find real happiness. 'I would like to come very much', I said.

I felt I was walking on air when I went back to college. I could face their amazement now. 'I've taken that grammar school job in the North', I said to my Principal. Now that the die was cast she was too kind to hold this against me.

'I can't imagine why, but I do hope you will be happy', she said.

I 'phoned my mother.

'Going North all that way?' she said unbelievingly. 'But why didn't you choose that other good job in Kent?' She was obviously sad.

'I'm so sorry, but I just had to. That's all.'

I felt as if my 'miracle' had happened, and now I would wait to see what it brought me.

12

THE NORTH

THE flat fields were racing past, half hidden in swirls of smoke from the engine, and the sky was getting greyer and had a cold look, when I gazed out of the window of the train heading north. Pressed into a corner seat, I had been contemplating the face of the lady opposite me. It was, somehow, encouraging. The expression was not sophisticated but kindly. She wore no make-up, and looked as if she confronted life fairly and squarely, and had little time or money to spend on luxuries. She was brisk, I thought, but sympathetic.

'Durham Cathedral!' She suddenly spoke, and her eyes lit up. The majestic outline, the stark magnificence in stone, rose out of the cliffside above the river on my right. I looked out, almost astonished.

'You know of it, of course', she added. 'Always a wonderful sight.'

'No. I've never seen it before.'

'Never seen it . . .' I was obviously a creature beyond her ken, and must be ignorant, or daft, perhaps. Then another thought came to her. She was both perplexed and curious.

'Are you a stranger to the north then?' she asked.

'Yes, it's my first journey here.'

Puzzled again, she gazed at me, and the next solution occurred to her.

'You'll be staying with friends, then, likely?'

'Well, no. I'm coming to a job.'

'A job! Ah well, you'll know people there.'

'No. Nobody really. It's a new job.'

113

The true northern kindness, which I was to come to know
well later, asserted itself. She leaned forward.

You look terribly young, then. What job are you going
to?'

'I'm going to teach. I named the school.'

It was then that my first 'thing' happened. Of all the
carriages I might have chosen at King's Cross, I had somehow arrived in the right one for me. For the unknown
traveller flung her hands in the air with a start of delighted
surprise.

'My own old school', she said, 'you will never find a better.'
She began to talk about it, telling of its long history in the
city.

A text leaped suddenly, unbidden, into my mind, just as
if my father was saying it himself, as he so often had, his
head lifted, and he gazing into the distance with the grave
light of pleasure in his eyes, his spirit sustained by the
thought of God's dealings with men:

'The Lord, he it is that doth go before thee; he will be
with thee, he will not fail thee.' This was a habit that returned to me from time to time in life, at moments of crisis
or perplexity, and I would seem to hear my father's calm
reassuring voice speaking the strong Biblical words, and my
timorous spirit would be strengthened.

Outside, the first signs of the real industrial north became
visible. The sky was darkening when I saw the great bridges
spanning the Tyne. The first sight of Newcastle, black and
forbidding, was a shock, although even in its gloom I felt
there was a certain sombre beauty. The river ran broad and
dark beneath us as we passed over the High Level Bridge,
and steamed slowly at a slackening speed. I looked out, even
more intently. The results of the terrible 'depression' still
obviously gripped the district. Almost appalled I watched an
endless vista of dreary streets, slate roofs and chimney pots,

partly shrouded in a pall of soot and smoke. The train slid gently to a stop.

Now the cavernous and draughty station increased the impression of bleakness, and I almost dreaded to leave the warmth and safety of the train carriage, but my new-found friend spoke kindly.

'I do hope you will soon find friends', she said, 'but here is my address if you are ever lonely. I should be really glad to see you, and we'll have a cup of tea.'

She gripped my hand, and vanished. It felt cold when she had gone.

Lights were starting to shine out from sad little shops, when I took a taxi which mounted a long hill, half of whose buildings were in a state of decay. Broken windows were stuffed with paper and rags, paint was peeling off doors, and there was a general air of poverty and desolation. Presently we left this area behind, and turned into a quiet faded district of monotonous streets and terraces of Victorian villas, their red brick dingy with the overall mask of soot.

The taxi stopped in front of a house exactly like every other in a long broad street. I was clearly in an area of faded respectability. Each house had a minute patch of sickly grass at the front, with perhaps a brave attempt at a few flowers beside it. But they did not bloom as at home. Instead, the murky air almost seemed to cast a blight on growth. Indeed the whole street looked dead. I rang the bell at the dark front door.

Mrs. Robson, who welcomed me in cheerfully and kindly, was clad in a sleeveless light summer dress I noted, as I stood shivering on the doorstep in my winter overcoat. I felt I had better toughen up to this chilly climate as quickly as possible, or like a hot house plant, I would speedily wither away in the chilly blast which I felt curling around my legs. Mrs. Robson took in two teachers to augment her husband's income which like that of so many men, was hard hit by the 'slump' on Tyneside.

I was shown to my bed sitting-room, which at that greying hour of the day, seemed rather cheerless as it looked out over slate roofs, chimney pots, and the back yard. After showing me 'the amenities' Mrs. Robson told me a little about the charming American teacher, who had now returned home, whose room I was about to inhabit, who had been literally the life and soul of the school and of this house. I felt I was obviously going to be a dreadful and disappointing anti-climax after this scintillating character.

'There is a cup of tea downstairs', Mrs. Robson said, and left me to my thoughts.

I stood in the middle of the room, and gazed distastefully at the rather ancient trunk I had brought, and wished ardently that I was a poised, sophisticated, glamorous person. Then I might make a success of the job. But in rude reality, I knew I was utterly 'green', and I had better do my best to disguise it. I put on some more lipstick, brushed my all too natural hair, took a deep breath, and descended the stairs, feeling a great despondency.

Nevertheless the tea was hot and cheering. It was brought into the little dining-room by a thin young maid. She was probably glad, I thought, to have a job like this, for it would give her food and keep and a small wage at a time when employment was often impossible to find.

Presently, I was joined by a lively red-haired girl with delicate features. She had, at the same time, a shrewd and capable look as if she could handle her life very competently. She gazed at me piercingly but kindly, and I felt I was being summed up and assessed. Mary taught at the same school, and was engaged to a curate in the city. She also had been to London University, but I was not surprised to find her home was in Yorkshire, for she had a certain robust attitude to life.

'Come and get warm', she said, holding out her hands to the rather small fire. Of course it was only September, but so far it felt like a Somerset mid-winter.

After tea Mary said she would give me 'the low down' on the school and all its characters. I listened, amused, to the vivid assessments of the various members of staff. This subsequently stood me in very good stead. It was a happy staff-room, and I slowly learned to be discreet with the die-hards, firm but polite with others, and not to relax except with those of like mind, and then we could 'let our hair down' together.

So my life in the North began. The first days passed in a dream. I was at first regarded as a complete Southerner, to be watched with suspicion as to my staying powers, and probably regarded as an inferior breed.

The Headmistress, however, showed great kindness and endless patience with all her young staff. I knew I was lucky to work for her, and I wanted to prove myself.

Mrs. Robson realised I was very homesick at first, and although she was a very kindly person, she obviously considered this to be a lack of stamina—indeed I felt it was almost an affront. Incredible as it now seems, we only paid thirty shillings a week for full board, and for this we certainly got good value, but no luxuries. From time to time when we longed for a night out, we would go off to the cinema and a café with one or two men from the nearby boys' school and life became more light-hearted.

Each morning I put on the Harris tweed costume my mother had anxiously insisted I should buy for the icy northern blasts, squared my shoulders and set off for the plain modern buildings of the school, rather like a pleasant factory, looking over its own playing fields. Mary found it almost impossible to get up in the mornings, and would come at a run a little behind me, often creeping very quietly

I

into the staff-room at the last minute, giving me a guilty wink as she tried to avoid being seen.

I found, almost to my surprise, that it was fun to teach a class of thirty lively intelligent girls who, amazingly, regarded me as a pillar of wisdom, and who quickly responded because I felt a genuine interest in them. I urged, exhorted, advised and cared for them, and in my own ears my voice sounded grimly hearty. By the end of the first week I had entirely lost my voice, and only a whisper came out, but they were most long-suffering until I recovered. From time to time it was all worthwhile, because we would burst out laughing together, and suddenly there was a firm bond between us, and I thought they were the nicest children in the world. I felt like one of them, and often had an insane desire to do something foolish.

The news from Germany grew daily worse. One evening there was the sound of shouting and general confusion in the street outside our 'digs'. Mary and I rushed to the front door. A man was shouting persistently through a huge megaphone. A large lorry was moving slowly down the street, and gas-masks were being handed out to every man, woman and child. The emergency was upon us, for this was the time of the Munich crisis. I remember a feeling of horror as I took my ugly mask from which, like everyone else, I was not to be parted for some years. When the crisis passed, and the Prime Minister, Neville Chamberlain, flew back from his talks with Hitler with the message that this meant 'peace in our time', we temporarily stifled our doubts and misgivings but not for long.

During this lull, while we went on with our everyday work, we knew full well that our future was becoming increasingly grave. Yet, like all young people, we made our own happiness, the keener perhaps because we had the feeling it could not last. We acted plays, had a badminton club, sometimes had small dances among ourselves, and often explored the countryside. We visited the church of the Venerable Bede at Jarrow and thought of the little boy, the only one, except for the Abbot, saved from the plague in the monastery where he grew up, who became England's first great historian and theologian. The rolling distances seen from Hadrian's Wall captured the imagination too, as one pictured the Roman legionaries shivering in their wind-swept guard posts.

Every weekend became memorable, because through the kindness of a friend at Cambridge, I was introduced to a Presbyterian minister on Tyneside, moderator of his church in England, who, with his wife, held open house for young people, as they had done for many years in Cambridge. They were an unusual lively family, and I never felt happier than when I was with them in the poor district which was now their home.

'You are our northern daughter', they sometimes said, and a warm glow went through me.

'Why did you come here?' I once asked the Minister. He was a scholar, but no less a shepherd to his flock, and had humour and wit.

'We had been so fortunate for so long that I just asked to be sent to the toughest place they could find," he answered, with a smile. 'So here I am.'

He was a man who, in a much greater way, felt what I had. I was encouraged.

I met other young people of my age at the manse. Yet for some reason I did not want to talk about my own home. I think that, foolishly, I dreaded people to think my parents were 'odd', fanatical, or religious extremists. I knew so well their simple goodness and dedication that I shrank from the unkind criticism of outsiders, of which I was often very conscious. How well I knew the surprised and, as I thought, scornful tones of some people who would say.

'You mean they are fundamentalists? Surely no intelligent people take that position now?' I knew my father was often misjudged because of his faith. I had once seen him hurt and angry because a certain doctor had advised a patient, against her strong wish, not to consult him.

'Certainly go to him if you want a prayer as well as a consultation!' he had said. Nothing could have been more unjust. My father was most scrupulous in observing medical etiquette, and never spoke of his Christian beliefs unless someone in need asked him. So while I might rebel against the Puritan setting of my home and could criticise it myself, I was not prepared to endure the harsh condemnation of others against my parents. I was too immature to realise that here, of all places, I would have got the sympathy and understanding I greatly wanted.

Equally, I was not willing to go my father's way. He had been anxious that I should find 'suitable' friends when I came north, and guessed I might be lonely. This irritated me.

'I'll make my own friends', I said impatiently, believing his ideas and mine would clash. However, he had insisted on writing to an old doctor friend of his, a Plymouth brother like himself, to ask him to have me to his home where he lived with his sister. Impatiently I had dismissed this idea. I wanted to start life afresh, and I felt it would not be within the fold of the Plymouth Brethren.

I believed my father was trying to draw me back in spirit to his way of thinking, and I was strongly resisting. I was quite frank with him about this.

'You know, Dad', I said one day when he was in a humorous mood, 'if ever I marry, which is very doubtful, it will never, never be to a Plymouth brother!'

'Well, don't protest so much', he said with a smile, 'or that's just what will happen.'

'Never!' I answered fervently.

When he tried to make this contact for me to have a home to go to if I was lonely, I rejected it entirely in my mind.

However, one Sunday I was at a loose end. The loneliness of a day with nowhere to go, and no one to talk to, rose up like a spectre before me. It was at such moments that a great longing for home would sweep over me. I gazed once again at a tiny card written in a crabbed spinsterish hand-writing which was propped up on the dressing-table in my rather drab room. I read over again the cordial invitation from the sister of my father's doctor friend to visit them and have lunch, any Sunday I liked, in their home in the country outside Newcastle. I turned it over and over thoughtfully. The view of slate roofs from my window was gloomy in the extreme. But white clouds were chasing across the cold blue sky, and a rough wind was rattling the glass panes. At all costs I wanted to get away for a few hours. On the spur of the moment, and almost unwillingly, I went downstairs and picked up the telephone.

So on that chilly Sunday morning, I sat once again in a little 'morning meeting' as the service was described. It was rather different from that at home. Here, in an old stone school-house in a country village, an upper room was the setting for a very small gathering of simple homely folk, who were all dominated by the dynamic character of the doctor. He was a man dedicated to his work of medicine, and loved in his district just as my father was. He had a strong noble face, which could have been arrogant and fierce if he had not been a Christian, but this impression was softened by the sudden amused smile. At all times among the Brethren he was the leader of his little band of saints, and he led them on, teaching them Sunday by Sunday, brooking no dispute or argument, sweeping them before him into the Kingdom of Heaven, the fruits of his ministry and trophies of grace.

When I met him and his sister before the meeting, I was, as at home—immediately enfolded into the love and warmth of a small community which cares deeply and intensely for its own. How could I be honest with them, I wondered, for although I could love them for their steady faith, I felt I could not be one of them at heart.

I gazed around the plain little room, with its wooden chairs set around a little central table, covered with a snowy white cloth, on which lay the bread and wine.

The hour of meditation, Bible reading and prayer was interspersed by an occasional hymn, unaccompanied by any organ or piano, until the Doctor rose, broke the loaf and poured the wine, and the sacrament was passed from hand to hand.

This little gathering, I felt, was impervious to the world which I loved and, in a sense, out of touch with life. Yet, as always, in face of their quiet and true devotion, my criticisms were silenced. I knew that for them, as for my father, this was the supreme hour of their week.

I had lunch with the Doctor and his sister in their quiet little house. As in many Plymouth Brethren homes there was, even then, a strong Victorian flavour. Furniture, ornaments, books were all reminiscent of past decades. Even the quiet young maid, her gold hair braided in plaits round her head, fitted exactly into this picture. She had set out for the meeting, large Bible clasped under her arm, and sat beside her mistress to whom she was devoted.

It was after lunch, as always preceded by quite a lengthy grace, that I had a surprise. I wondered what I would do during the afternoon. I had seen a number of devotional books and magazines in the drawing room; *The Life of Faith*, *Echoes of Service*, *The Witness*, *The Harvester*. My spirit quailed.

An afternoon with *The Witness* was a formidable thought. Then the Doctor's sister, with gentle courtesy, laid her hand on my arm and spoke.

'Now dear, it's such a pleasure to have you, and we want you to stay to tea. But as we old folks are going to rest now, here are some magazines for you.' She turned to a cupboard. I feared the worst. Instead, with a gentle smile, she brought out an armful of the latest numbers of *Punch*. I heaved a sigh of relief. Most brethren households never read any secular literature whatever on Sunday, and I felt a concession had been made.

When I was leaving, just after tea, the old doctor gripped my hand. The genuine pleasure he showed at having me brought an absurd lump into my throat, and I tried to thank him for his hospitality.

'Anne,' he said, 'you know I'm afraid we're much too old for you. I am going to write to a family a few miles away where there are young people of your own age.'

'Oh dear,' I thought, 'they are trying to draw me back. What shall I do?' I made some non-committal reply and thought I probably would not go again.

It was not until the next term that again an empty Sunday loomed ahead. Again, and in a way unwillingly and almost surprised at myself, I took the rattling tram down the steep hill to catch a train to the little country station. I gazed, as always with sadness, at the terrible slums near the railway on the first part of the journey. It really was a depressing area. If only, I thought, I could be looking at the little fields, the scented gardens, and the heavy blossom of the fruit trees at home. I often wondered what had made me come so far away. I supposed it was all good experience. In any case, I believed our lives would soon alter drastically, for it seemed that war was getting very close. If it came, the school was destined to be evacuated and go west to an unknown destination. Life was all uncertain. Meantime, I would write and tell my father I had gone to see the Doctor again, for that would please him. It was for my father's sake I was going back again really, for I suspected I was not 'one of them'.

I went up the bare wooden stairs to the upper room. The 'saints' were sitting quietly meditating, some with their Bibles open on their knees. I had the same welcome at the door where the Doctor was greeting one and another of his little flock. As before, I went over to sit by his sister, and their pleasure at seeing me was both genuine and touching.

Quiet meditation had never been easy for me. My eyes roved restlessly around the simple uncluttered room, and suddenly, I saw three people unknown to me, sitting opposite. First I gazed at a distinguished looking elderly man. He looked a man of culture and quiet dignity; his appearance was rather military, and he sat very erect. He was tall, thin and clean shaven with a close-cropped grey moustache. He seemed to look a little sad as he gazed away from his open Bible to some distant place where his thoughts were wandering. Beside him sat a tall and beautiful girl with strikingly lovely brown eyes, which had a hint of humour in them. Next to her was a young man, obviously her brother. He, too, was tall and dark, and was sitting as if lost in his own thoughts. His expression was firm and grave, and gave me the idea that he was used to looking over long distances to far horizons. Just then he had a serene look as if he could shut out the world at will.

Presently he looked at me with a slightly questioning glance.

'Yes, you may well wonder what I am doing here,' I thought idly, 'but I'm curious to know how you fit in.'

It eventually turned out that I was seeing for the first time the family whom the Doctor so much wanted me to meet.

13

THE LONG SUMMER

THE long hot summer of 1939 wore on. It was August and I was sitting with two friends from school days in the train heading for Penzance. We had written to a small guest house situated on the extreme western tip of Cornwall, and here we planned to stay together for a fortnight before Mary got married, and Margaret and I returned to our separate teaching posts.

Sitting in the Cornish Riviera express we had gazed out at the neat fields and hedgerows, rather like a chess board, of Somerset and Devon, intimate cosy country where the earth changed from warm brown to red and the land was rich and lush. I found myself comparing it with the endless moors of the north country stabbed by the brilliant gold of gorse and broom in summer, the far distant horizon, the peculiar quality of the pale clear light which seemed to accentuate the windy spaciousness of the rough land which lay open and unsheltered under the vault of the sky. A hard and demanding place. Travelling to Cornwall was a return to the familiar, the homely and dearly loved, where, as the railway edged along the Atlantic coast, the beauty often lay in the meeting of sea and cliffs and rocks.

After leaving the train, we journeyed by bus to a tiny village, perched near the cliff edge. The guest house, an old low stone farmhouse, was pleasant and unimposing, its windows looked across the rolling waters of the Atlantic. We were shown to one long low bedroom with a big bed, a smaller bed, and a still smaller bed.

'They must be expecting the three bears', said Margaret, as we drew lots for the biggest.

125

From the window we gazed out over the deep blue water, idly watching the foam-topped waves surge up and vanish from sight beneath the cliff. We were aware of a perpetual tapping in the next bedroom. Later, a middle-aged lady with wiry hair emerged, and gazed at us out of unseeing eyes, where we stood on the landing. We soon found out that she was the authoress of very 'purple' romantic novels, and even now was bringing to birth another, for it was her loud typewriter that clacked away into the midnight hours. I wondered what romance had touched her own life, for as she vaguely fluttered round with haggard expression, and different gauze scarves wound round her neck each day, which floated wispily out behind, she somehow did not give an impression of personal involvement. Perhaps her books are the outlet for a frustrated life, I thought.

We settled down for two weeks as we thought, but the daily news became increasingly menacing. Life was punctuated by loud voices from the crackling radio, issuing orders, recalling troops, instructing Civil Defence personnel, warning teachers in evacuation areas to listen for possible instruction, and advising reputedly safe areas to have all plans ready for the mass evacuation of children from danger zones.

By the second evening I was waiting tensely to see what orders might come through for me, and felt our holiday might end before it had begun. Together we walked rather sadly along the cliff path to the tiny white coastguard station. We stopped to talk to the burly cheerful man on duty. Steady and unruffled he was gazing out to sea through a large telescope, turning from side to side to watch for the slightest strange speck on the surface of the water.

'Nearly on us now, I reckon', he said without fuss or preamble. 'Any minute now the balloon's going up.' He was steady and 'unflappable', and I was sure the soft Cornish voice hid a dogged character. Hitler might well find us a tougher race to subdue than he bargained for, I thought, when in every town and village, calm staunch characters like this waited defiantly.

I shivered as we walked back to the little farm guest house in the gathering darkness. Would a vast armada of bombers and warships move against us without warning, I wondered. As we entered the kitchen, just before nine o'clock, there was an air of suppressed excitement. About a dozen people were clustered round the wireless, including farm workers, the novelist, and as far as I could guess, anyone who had felt like dropping in from the village to discuss the situation. The proprietress turned to me.

'Your message came through on the six o'clock, dear,' she said, 'all teachers recalled at once.' Suddenly the scene became almost too vivid, so that I felt I would never forget it. The clustered figures, half hidden in pipe smoke, the bright scarlet of geraniums on the window sill, the shabby harmonium, the shaft of silver light which crossed and re-crossed the ceiling, coming from a searchlight on the cliffs, repeated on the grand scale as it passed relentlessly across the night sky outside, made an unforgettable picture—a farewell scene to life as I have known it, I thought. The deep echoing voice of Big Ben sounded the hour, and I listened, almost rigid, to my instructions.

The next morning we climbed back on to the express train, the first of the day. Margaret and Mary felt they must get home too. This time, the train was packed with troops, young soldiers of the Territorial and Regular Armies rejoining their units. I was wedged in the crowded corridor, at one point, beside a young lieutenant. His handsome public-school face had a slightly apprehensive expression; he smoked cigarette after cigarette, and was clearly doing his best to hide his feelings. We talked a little.

'Please will you come and have a cup of coffee in the restaurant car?' he said. He seemed as if he wanted a human contact in a world that was going mad. Now one might grasp at anyone or anything for comfort, just as a drowning man seizes at any bit of flotsam drifting on the sea.

The journey was hot and tedious. Margaret and I arrived at tea-time, and gravely said goodbye on the station platform, wondering if our paths would cross again. We had shared fun and laughter together, and it was good, now, to remember that. Mary was going on to London.

I took a bus to my home. My mother had a meal ready, and had found the time of the night train to Newcastle. She had busied herself by starting to pack for me. They were obviously distressed. My father was a semi-invalid, and said he felt useless in this emergency.

'I am just a burden to others now', he said. This was so unlike his usual serenity. The house seemed different, tin helmets stood on the hall table, gas masks lay in the sitting room. I noticed large red buckets of sand here and there. For incendiary bombs I suppose, I thought—they surely don't think they will drop here. I could not foresee how utterly wrong I was to be proved. It was certain that everyone expected the onslaught at any minute if Hitler pursued his normal tactics.

'I'm so thankful you are getting all the children out of the danger zone', said my mother.

'Well, I'd rather join the w.r.n.s.', I said bluntly.

'Don't be foolish. This job is both vital and constructive.' My father, in his anxiety, started a little lecture. I looked at them helplessly. They seemed so frail to leave, although I knew they both had unfailing courage in any emergency.

The dreaded moment of departure came, and the one thought uppermost in my mind was, would I see them again? The taxi waited at the door, its engine running. I could not keep it waiting for there were many in the city who were setting out on journeys that night.

My father looked at me, and gripped my hand. He was smiling as if to encourage me, but because of the sadness in his eyes I could not speak.

We left my home at seven o'clock. My mother who had come to see me off, waved until the train turned the bend, and I could see her no longer. I watched the golden sunset turning to pale yellow and then a delicate green with silver streaks across it. Then as darkness fell, the first stars came out, and the carriage grew darker and darker. It was with a shock that I realised we were only allowed one tiny dark blue light, so that one was only vaguely aware of the dim outline of other figures. All blinds were drawn, and I felt almost claustrophobic in the cramped space. A young soldier, a territorial, in obviously new uniform, was seated next to me, and had been travelling a long time. He fell asleep on my shoulder. I grew stiff and uncomfortable but did not like to wake him. In sleep he looked innocent and defenceless, a farm boy, perhaps, his fair hair ruffled, his cheeks rosy.

We arrived, at last, in Newcastle, in the clear grey light of a northern morning. The barrage balloons were flying high.

The nightmare of the long wait began. Only a few days in reality, it seemed so long it was like being poised on the edge of eternity. No final orders to evacuate came through, and so in the warm days of late August, when the children should have been happily playing on the beaches or in the summer fields, we were instructed to keep them in school for a time each day, and teach or amuse them, so that they would be ready and mobile to move off on the instant. Above all, we were to keep up morale and foster cheerfulness.

I organised endless games, competitions, quizzes in English lessons, drama groups, anything that would bring a smile to their faces which were beginning to show signs of strain and, even, in some cases, fear.

Outside, formations of bombers and fighters roared past above us from time to time. Inside, the staff room was thick with the smoke of endless cigarettes. Everyone talked quietly, and we all tried to ease the tension, it seemed, by being extra courteous and considerate.

Our headmistress, of whom we were all fond—she was all I had imagined her to be—had a heavy burden; for all the girls would be her responsibility in what we believed might be very difficult circumstances. She talked calmly and unemotionally with us, outlining plans as far as she was free to do so. She had been ill and in hospital for a long spell that year, and the lines on her face betrayed the tension she never showed. Whenever she could joke with us, she did, and when a child was upset she was encouraging and sympathetic with her. On the whole the fortitude of the children was beyond praise.

Mary, who had shared my 'digs', was no longer with us. She had married her curate in the summer, and they had a little house in a rather poor district of Newcastle, where he worked. Now I grew to know the young science mistress better. She had been at my own college at London University, so there was a bond at the beginning. Short and square, cheerful, kind and practical, and with a rock-like dependability, she was good company, and an invaluable person in a crisis. She was known by staff and girls as 'Tim', and we often talked together during this time and wondered what the future—if any—might bring. The time dragged on.

One day the Head came out of her room, a sheaf of papers in her hand. One look at her, and we guessed that she carried the news for which we had been waiting. Quietly she told us to gather the children in the Assembly Hall. The silence was almost dreadful as we all listened to our orders. We were to assemble at a certain school in the city centre early the next morning, carrying light cases only, our gas masks, and enough food for the day.

I looked at the childrens' faces as at last it came home to them that now they must really leave their parents behind. As for us, we would have to become parent, friend and general comforter overnight, so I smiled at my twelve year olds, hoping to indicate that this adventure would be fun, although I felt that was the last thing it might be.

'Well, here goes!' I said, 'Chins up! Who knows what adventures may not come our way?'

They laughed, and almost affectionately one said, 'Don't forget your gas mask, will you?'

No one slept well that night I believe.

The grey dawn came at last, bringing a chill Northumbrian mist at first. I met Tim, and together we made our way to the large barrack-like city school, through streets full of hundreds and hundreds of children in uniform, walking hurriedly from all directions to the various centrally-sited schools where they had been ordered to gather. Many parents walked with them. Often we smiled or waved a hand as one of our own children passed us. Already there was a strong feeling of comradeship.

On arrival, we each welcomed our own groups of thirty to thirty-five children, ticking off their names on lists. We were as gay as it was possible to be, teasing the cheerful, consoling the timid, trying to make each child feel she now belonged to one large safe family, for only so could this experience leave her unscathed.

We paced up and down the corridor by the few classrooms allotted to the hundreds of children from our own girls' school and boys' school, wondering how long the intolerable wait would be prolonged. Sometimes we gazed out of the windows observing the staff from other schools with dispassionate interest. Large plump motherly women hustled tiny infant-school children along, whose heads were almost dwarfed by the cardboard boxes of their gas masks which bobbed along on their backs. Quiet withdrawn men, rather too old for call-up, often with pipes clenched between teeth, ambled impatiently up and down watching the far noisier grammar school boys as they stamped and shuffled impatiently in the rooms allotted to them. Occasionally a violent shouting would be heard as a master called his tribe to order.

The second mistress came to each one of us, checking and re-checking the lists of names. It seemed eternity that we were imprisoned in this place with nothing whatever to do. So we went through every game we could play without moving, 'I spy', 'Vegetable and Mineral', 'O'Grady says' . . .

At last there was a sudden stir, a breath of excitement. Anxious-looking city officials and education officers passed from one Head to another and spoke rapidly. A deathly silence fell. Suddenly we heard the clear Scottish voice of the second mistress, 'Form up two by two, starting with the Upper VIth, and follow me calmly and quietly—with no running. We are now going to walk to the Central Station.' There was a sound, wordless, almost like a sigh, then a great shuffling of feet and we were off.

As we came outside, a watery sun was just trying to pierce through the morning mists, and we saw a dramatic sight. Endless crocodiles of children were passing quietly through the streets, many parents walking alongside them as if they could not bear to let them go. Yet I saw no tears, no panic. There was an indefinable air of complete defiance. Even our children were unconquerable I thought, as I smiled at my form, and they flashed back instant smiles, as if to say,

'We won't let you down.' And so with heads up, and facing an unknown future, the children left the city.

'It became like a city of the dead overnight,' one who was left behind told me, and who knows what grief thousands of parents endured that day?

14

3 SEPTEMBER 1939

THE long train very slowly steamed westwards. It seemed as if one of England's most ancient engines had been hauled out of obscurity for this job. A hot sun now shone into the carriages packed with sticky weary children. Sandwiches and sweets were finished, and no one knew what home they would have that night.

It was mid afternoon when at last the train appeared to hesitate and finally stopped at the small station of a little market town in Cumberland, and stiff and weary, a seething mass of children flowed out onto the platform.

A rather formidable plump rosy-cheeked lady, her hat perched firmly and squarely on top of grey hair done in a large bun at the back, waited to meet us. This was the head-mistress of the girls' grammar school which we were officially to share. She literally swooped down on our own poor tired Head like some bird of prey, almost propelling her along, and beckoning to us all to follow. Streaming along in her wake, we tramped down the country lanes which were thick with white dust, and splashed with dung from market day, and followed her to a red brick building, faced with stone, shaded by tall trees with a large orchard beside it. We were swept into the orchard, where harassed officials standing around under the apple trees, vaguely waved their arms to indicate we might sit. They gazed at us helplessly as we thronged wearily onto the grass, filling the orchard to overflowing. As there were no seats, the children flung themselves down dispiritedly on the grass, their fears now lively within them as to where they would be sent.

134

Now a great cluster of townspeople came forward into the orchard, ready to pick a child or two to take home. This was a terrible process. The happy extrovert children gazing around with friendly smiles were inevitably taken first. Our Head and her deputy desperately tried to keep track of every child and the address to which she was going. But such was the confusion that it often seemed likely that determined hostesses would simply bear the girls off to an unknown destination. This we had to prevent.

As we stood, checking the fate of each girl in our own form, we realised with growing horror that many children were in danger of having nowhere to go, that there were not enough billets for them, that somewhere the organisation was falling down. Those who were left clustered close to us, pale and sometimes tearful, the fear of being unwanted beginning to flood over them.

Evacuation officials almost tore their hair as they studied lists, conferred, rushed out into the little town again in desperate attempts to find more billets. From time to time they gazed at us in despair which almost mounted to dislike at this violent intrusion into their peaceful existence. The local Headmistress came forward with suggestions, and plans of campaign, and the team of helpers battled on, in what seemed at times a hopeless task. Presently various public-spirited and motherly women arrived at the orchard, having heard of the childrens' plight, to say they would try and 'squeeze one more in, but just for the night'.

Our head grew steadily more pale and tired. Her own health was far from good, and the nightmare of the girls' predicament was obviously a dreadful responsibility, although she never lost her calmness and resolution.

As the long late summer afternoon wore on, I began to wonder where the staff might go. Then I was introduced to a dear little plump lady with a warm motherly smile. Mrs.

Moffat explained she was anxious to take in two teachers, as she had a weak heart, and felt she was past taking in children. I threaded my way through the still crowded orchard to find 'Tim'.

'I've been offered a billet for two teachers. Would you like to come and see Mrs. Moffat. It sounds nice.'

Tim had been wearily coping with her form of senior girls, and they still had not all been settled. Someone took over from her. Mrs. Moffat insisted on taking us down the road a short way, and turned into a neat front garden, up two or three stone steps into a pillared portico. Her home was a solid square Cumbrian house, with red sandstone lintels over the door and windows. It was cool and quiet inside after the milling crowds at the school.

We were introduced to 'David', her husband. He was elderly, with grizzled grey hair, very piercing dark brown eyes, and a sudden wicked smile, the smile of a born comedian. One could imagine him, in youth, leaping onto a stage on Blackpool pier, and cracking outrageous jokes or singing sentimental songs.

Mrs. Moffat could not rest until she had taken us upstairs.

'There's just the one room I can give you,' she said anxiously, 'but it's clean and comfortable. I'm afraid there's only the one double bed, but it's got a good feather mattress. Perhaps you could manage?'

Tim and I looked at each other, and I felt inclined to laugh. A double feather bed seemed to me a peculiarity indeed, but if the war brought us nothing worse, we would be very fortunate. Indeed, the bed was a noble solid iron structure, with large brass knobs. We gazed at the cool, spotlessly clean room, with its shining patterned lino, and the pleasant view of a neat garden at the back, looking across acres of fields to the distant fells of Cumberland. Suddenly the peace of it all seemed heaven, and I knew we were both inexpressibly weary. Tim nodded at me.

'Thank you so much, it's lovely', we said.

Mrs. Moffat, beaming in the motherly way that was to become so endearing to us, told us there would be a good meal ready when we were free. As she went downstairs I turned and said to Tim,

'We can always put a bolster down the middle, so I don't kick you out.'

Before we went, Mrs. Moffat insisted on leading us to a large fading photograph in the front sitting room. It was a very young stocky soldier, cheerful and smiling, ready to set out for the front in the first World War.

'That's our David. He was killed in the last War. Our only child. So we know what you are feeling.' Her eyes filled with tears for a moment.

Back in the orchard, we found order was very slowly emerging out of the confusion. But it was not until darkness fell that the last child had been found a temporary home.

It was past midnight before I climbed into my side of the feather bed, and sank down and down. It was like floating on a soft cloud. Tim was already asleep, breathing deeply, but the long hard bolster between us, and our own tiredness prevented us from finding the bed too strange. I was drowsily conscious of the smell of roses, hay and cut grass drifting in through the window. Vaguely I wondered what was happening under the barrage balloons in Newcastle.

A lonely plane on a night mission droned overhead.

Then I slept . . .

It seemed only a few minutes later, when I suddenly woke with a sense of urgency and heard loud martial music coming from a very powerful wireless in the room beneath.

'The war!' I thought, and leaped out of bed as if a bomb had dropped. I pulled up the navy blue blind, only to see the fields bathed in sunshine and the countryside lying peaceful and quiet, as if yesterday had been all a bad dream. Tim was still deeply unconscious. I shook her.

'Wake up, it must be awfully late. Do you think it's begun yet?'

Tim groaned, rolled over, looked at her watch.

'Ye Gods, it's half past nine. We have to be there at ten.' The bed heaved, and she surfaced from the depths of the feather mattress, and gazed at me as if she had forgotten why we were in this place.

'It seems so odd and quiet here, like being cast up on a desert island,' I said, as I brushed my hair and gazed into the mirror, surprised to find I was looking the same as usual, and refreshed after a night's sleep.

Mrs. Moffat gave us a large breakfast and appeared only anxious to mother us, and feed us up.

When we arrived at the school, we had a day full of problems. Some of the girls were happy and came to tell us how they had got on.

'It's smashing, they let us do just as we like. We had a lovely supper,' was one comment.

But there were tears from others who had not been fortunate, and who realised they were not wanted in their new homes.

'There were four of us in one bed and we couldn't sleep at all,' one child told us.

'She gave us chips for supper and nothing else, not even bread', was another story.

'She says she can't do with me. Please could I go home?' This last was accompanied by bitter crying from a shaken child.

Story after story had to be patiently listened to, the truth sifted out, and then the billet had to be visited, also those organising the evacuation had to be interviewed. Our Head began to walk the streets of the little town herself, looking for any new suitable home that could be found for this girl and that. This we all did in the ensuing days.

We were allotted a living space in the school which, from then on, was to be the only place where we could gather our forms. Mine was the balcony of the Assembly Hall. Here, as it were, we took up residence, for classroom space was totally inadequate, and the rightful school was to use their building for the first half of each day. We were to learn to adapt ourselves to any situation, any inconvenience, any lack of space, of books, and of materials, and to rely on initiative alone. Before the evacuation was ended I had taught lessons in so many extraordinary corners, including a large cupboard, that I felt nothing could disturb me again. But at this stage we did not know what was to come.

The next day was Sunday, although by then we had lost all count of time. We were told to assemble with the girls outside the Parish Church for the morning service. The boys' school joined us, and together we filled the church to over-flowing. The children, who were very quiet, were slowly trying to settle down. Some were even hoping their parents would come over and see them that day.

As we streamed out into the sunshine, the School Secretary, a tall handsome girl, who had worked unflaggingly over the evacuation plans, came up and spoke to us.

'It's begun,' she said. 'The ultimatum has expired and we're at war. The Prime Minister has been speaking over the radio, and the air raid sirens have sounded in Newcastle.' She spoke quietly, but her expression was strained. Her fiancé was in the Royal Navy, and she would have little peace of mind from then on.

Now that all hope was gone, it was, oddly, almost a relief to hear the worst, and to know that we must brace ourselves for whatever might come.

That Sunday evening I walked out through the fields and

thought over the last few months of the summer in New-castle. Rather to my own surprise, I had been out a number of times to the home of the family to whom the old Doctor had introduced me. Elizabeth was a beautiful girl, and talented at music. She had a lively sense of humour, and because of our upbringing there were many jokes we could share. She looked after the home and her father, as her mother had died when she was little more than a baby.

Tom, her brother, was not often at home, but when he came I found him interesting. He was a lawyer, practising some distance away, and seemed to lead a full life. He was an excellent horseman, was fond of sailing and canoeing, drove an M.G. sports car, and seemed to lead a full and satisfying life. Then why, I asked myself, was he so relaxed and serene when he was home on a Sunday, and went to the 'morning meeting' with his father, a staunch and sometimes strict Plymouth Brother like my father, albeit a man of great courtesy and charm? Tom did not seem to rebel against his puritan upbringing as I did. In some way he seemed to understand the best in it, and to absorb it. This, I felt impatiently, I could not do. Yet, I suspected he was not in complete agreement with it. I wanted to know more.

Somehow I had felt easy with him, because now I could talk freely about my own home, and he understood perfectly, and did not think it odd or repellent, because it was, in many ways, like his own. I had been out with him alone two or three times, but I thought I would probably not see him again. I was angry at feeling sad. 'If you want nothing but fun and gaiety, then he's not the sort of person to think about', I said to myself.

But deep in my heart I knew that was not all I wanted.

Quickly I turned my thoughts to how I had satisfied a long-held ambition, and had learned to ride that spring and summer. One evening each week I had gone off to a riding school just outside the city. Here in the acres of fields surrounding an old farm house, I had been taught by an impatient Irish instructor, who was a great teacher because nothing slipshod or unsatisfactory passed him.

'Rise in your stirrups now, grip with your knees, don't be like a sack of coals!' he would say. As I rhythmically rose and fell, I was conscious of the sweet scent of the hay fields and the hedges of May, mingled with the strong smell of horse and leather. I wanted to satisfy my craving for excitement by galloping before I could trot, but we were well disciplined and it seemed a long time before I was allowed to give the horse his head. Then the pleasure was acute and my spirit raced with the thudding hoofs.

As I thought over these things, I knew that I had come to love the North, but my own personal conflicts I still could not solve.

The days passed slowly. I found I thought often of all the people who had been so kind to me in Newcastle.

'This is a grim time', wrote the Presbyterian minister. His house was empty and quiet, his four children evacuated, and he added, 'We miss the children beyond words.'

Very often, in the evenings I would bicycle down the country lanes, and generally went towards the coast. Sometimes I would stand gazing out over the grey tossing waters of the Solway Firth when the tide raced in across the mud flats. I loved to watch the changing evening light on the distant hills, and I wanted to think. I found I was waiting for something—I did not know what.

It was a restless uneasy time. The war seemed static, but many of our friends and acquaintances were going away.

Sometimes I thought of my father. I could not always agree with him, and yet, again and again, I had seen him bring hope and peace where there was despair. I thought of Tom who seemed unmoved by what men thought of him, and whose faith, I believed, was firm and sure.

One evening, I found myself gazing at a rush-fringed pool. The golden light of the sunset was so bright that the water had become a mirror of its brilliance, and a poem came slowly into my head. I went home and wrote it down:

> 'The light of evening burnishes the pool,
> Shimmering the surface. Smoothly glistening,
> Reflecting back the sky, yet quiet, cool,
> It lies remote from the world's mad onrush,
> And seems at peace through quiet listening
> To secret voices: water's soft murmur,
> Or echoing night sounds dwindling to their hush.
> Pause, now, and still the heart,
> Quiet the tumult of the anxious mind.
> See how the work of God, untouched by man,
> Tells us of that true peace which all may find.
> Just as the pool reflects the evening light,
> So can a man, whose face is turned to God
> Illumine all his passing earthly span,
> Amidst the chaos of the world's dark night.'

It was not very good, but I was glad to put it on paper. Perhaps, at last, I was beginning to be honest with myself.

Some days later I walked home dispiritedly. Life seemed flat and stale. The constant effort to keep up the childrens' spirits in school, sometimes left us tired.

I walked into the homely kitchen, where a fire was burning. It was good to drink the hot sweet tea that was waiting, to sit and gaze into the glowing coals. Mrs. Moffat came in with her beaming smile.

'Have you looked at the mantelpiece?' she said.

I looked up, not knowing what she meant, and saw a fat letter addressed to me. In an instant I was out of the chair, and had torn the envelope open. I was conscious of no one around me.

Tom was writing to tell me all that had happened to him. He had joined seamanship classes in Newcastle and had gained his Yachtmaster's Certificate. He hoped his call-up would be soon, and that he would eventually get into minesweepers. Meanwhile, he was Commandant of the Auxiliary Fire Service and had been chasing round the country extinguishing burning hay-stacks.

I read the last sentence over and over again: 'Please do write and tell me all about yourself, and keep in touch.'

A new energy suddenly seized me.

'Have you any ink, Tim?' I said, seizing some notepaper.

Tim raised her eyebrows, and looked at me quizzically.

'Well, well, well,' she said, handing over the bottle, 'Don't use it all up!'

When I walked to the Post Office late the next evening, I found myself whistling a gay tune. Turning the corner, I suddenly came face to face with our Headmistress. She looked amused.

'How nice to hear someone who is happy again!' she said smiling.

Later, I thought about this. Yes, just then I was happy. I had a strange feeling that whatever ordeal might lie ahead, I would at last find the way home.

15

FIRE AT NIGHT

THE wheel had come full circle. I thought that by going North, I would solve my problems in my own way, and would find out how to break free from the embracing love and hidden power that the Brethren had over me. Now I had to face the surprising, almost alarming, fact that I was falling in love with a man who, brought up as I had been, apparently felt no such need to make a break, seeing good in this—to me—strict and demanding fellowship of Christians; a man who yet enjoyed all the normal and legitimate pleasures of life which I loved.

It was almost humorous. The very situation I had determined never to experience, now faced me, and I was moving relentlessly into a position from which I felt sure there would be no retreat. I sensed instinctively that there was in Tom, as in my father, that ultimate 'withdrawn-ness' from the world, that austerity, that deep loneliness of spirit arising from an undeviating purpose. I knew well that no woman would come first in the life of such a man, and I would have to be content for his vocation, whatever it was, to be of prime importance.

Governed, as always, by the heart rather than the head, I did not entirely face up to this. I felt that I had found the one person with whom I could be myself, because he understood and sympathised with my background and home. For some reason this seemed of great importance.

In a way I was lost and blinded to analytical thought. Tom was unusually handsome, and I was proud when on rare occasions he was free to take me out, and sighs of envy arose from various friends. I did not look far enough ahead to wonder what problems confronted us. I was content to enjoy the present and anything it might offer.

Our future seemed very uncertain, and we were only able to meet at infrequent and brief intervals, short inadequate meetings, and then suddenly the smouldering 'phoney' war, as it was called, burst into such a fury and holocaust that one's plans seemed totally insignificant, unlikely ever to be achieved, and the nightmare days of 1940 and 1941 darkened our lives. To live through that time was to have the memory seared by events that were pictured indelibly in the mind.

Looking back now from the comparative peace of the 1960's, even in a world sickened by war in Vietnam and elsewhere, one realises that almost nothing that has happened since stands out quite so vividly in the memory as those days twenty seven years ago. Once again I can walk through streets littered with glass, where the remains of blackened gaunt buildings gape in ruins; I can watch the tremendous upward-pluming clouds of dust as towering unsafe walls are demolished by the army; I can see little families pushing handcarts and prams and boxes on wheels containing all that is left of their worldly possessions, trying to find some hall or reception centre where they may wait in hope for day after day, until they can find any place to live.

The Blitz was upon us in all its horror. But at first we were cut off from the dramatic events in the south of England. We had been re-evacuated to the tiny picturesque town of Ambleside, in the Lake district, set in the heart of the mountains. Life had an air of unreality as day after day we listened to the news of the German armies sweeping across Europe towards the Channel, and then listened with mounting apprehension to the great drama of Dunkirk. As summer turned into autumn and the hills glowed with the gold and brown and red colours of September and October, we heard of the massive air raids on London and the ports. It irked the spirit to be so remote and cut off. Yet from time to time there were compensations.

When winter came at last, it was severe. The thermometer fell steeply. After the gripping cold and frost the lanes and field paths became as hard as iron, and the mountain peaks were capped with snow. A soft film of silver lay over the grass and trees. Then late one afternoon a sighing moaning wind blew over the hills from the east, and as we hurried down the hill from the school to the little hotel where three of us were billeted, the air was full of whirling snowflakes that clung to the face and hair and clothes as tiny drops of icy moisture.

It snowed steadily all night. In the morning we found ourselves in an enchanted snow-covered land, where the lakes were frozen, and the mountains shone dazzling white in the golden sunshine of morning. It was a Saturday, and we borrowed sledges and tin tea-trays, and on the lower mountain slopes made a swift exciting toboggan run. For a few days we became children again, shouting and laughing as we raced over the hard icy tracks.

One night an unusually brilliant full moon rose slowly and majestically over the tops of the peaks. We decided to climb a mountain in the softly glowing silvery light. As we climbed up the rough slopes, the crisp snow crackled beneath our feet, and, awestruck, we looked out over range after range of cold white dazzling peaks outlined against the dark star-studded sky. An owl flew heavily out of a copse of fir trees, its wings slowly and deliberately beating against the icy air. In the distance sheep called occasionally from the lower pastures, and somewhere away beneath us a lonely dog barked in his cold farmyard. The solemn splendour of this

scene seemed like a mighty backcloth for the drama of man's
eternal dilemma as he searched in vain for peace.

It was shortly after this that I was due for a brief holiday
at home. As usual I travelled by night arriving home in time
for breakfast, and passing through Birmingham and Bristol
after the spasmodic night raids were over.

The beautiful city of Bath, at this time, harboured many
strangers and refugees, driven from other places by the
war. At about this time, while at home, I went to visit my
mother who was in hospital for a few days. As I left the
building after seeing her, I flung open the swing doors which
led outside, and came face to face with a very small per-
sonage. I hastily drew back, holding open the door for him,
but he bowed very low, smiled gently and indicated that he
had no intention of entering until he had allowed me to pass
first. I gazed fascinated at the thick soft black hair framing
the olive-coloured aristocratic face, and received instantly
such an impression of splendid 'goodness' that it was like
encountering an angelic being unexpectedly in the middle of
Oxford Street. So I came face to face with Haile Selassie,
Emperor of Ethiopia, Lion of Judah . . . Not long afterwards
my parents were invited to meet him at tea with a well
known Quaker Doctor and his wife. They described his deep
and quiet courtesy, his charm and simplicity, and all together they discussed the faith they held dear, for he was a
dedicated and convinced Christian.

I had only been home a few days, a peaceful undisturbed
week, meeting friends, wandering through all the old haunts
in the city I loved, browsing in the bookshops, and listening
to the wonderful playing of Dame Myra Hess at a special
wartime concert, when the air raid siren was heard once
or twice during the day. Nothing apparently happened.

Late in the evening when darkness had fallen I was sitting
with my parents in front of the fire, reading. Once more the

wail of the Siren was heard rising and falling like a mournful despairing lamentation. In a few moments there came the dreaded sound of enemy planes passing steadily and relentlessly overhead. For a long time we listened but there was no sound of bombs being dropped. Our lights were dimmed, the heavy shutters closed and the blackout curtains secured.

After a time, my mother, obviously on edge and tense, looked up from her sewing and said, 'What can be happening? The sky sounds full of them.'

The very air seemed to be vibrating with the heavy uneven drumming note.

'Let's turn out all the lights and look out of the front door', I said.

It was a mild damp night for that time of year, the moon not yet up, and all should have been dark and still. But when the door was opened we saw a terrible sight. The great vault of the sky was lit up by a lurid flickering red glare, against which trees and buildings were silhouetted in black outline.

'It's Bristol', said my mother, almost in a whisper, 'they've set fire to it and soon the bombing will begin.' We felt stunned as we gazed at the brilliant glow, and ever and again great leaping flames writhed up and fell back, only to flare up with renewed strength.

'Better get inside', I said. My mother often seemed quite oblivious of personal danger.

We went back into the room where my father was reading. He looked up calmly and questioningly.

'Bristol is on fire,' I said, 'the whole sky is alight. I'm sure there's going to be a terrible raid.'

My father sighed, put down the current number of the British Medical Journal, and picked up his Bible. My stepsister lived in Bristol and would be fire-watching at that very time.

At that moment a violent thud shook the house, and the flap of the metal letter-box in the front door began to rattle. High up above us, it sounded as if the German raiders were now passing over in even increasing numbers. The unmistakeable halting note of their engines could always be recognised. Another thud was heard, and an answering roar from the anti-aircraft guns echoed along the hills. Very soon, over toward Bristol, the sound of ceaseless bombing began. The ground was shaken by the reverberating explosions; to think of all those directly beneath this onslaught destroyed one's calm, and sapped all feeling except that of horror at humanity's plight, when men deliberately set out to kill the innocent.

At length my father spoke quietly and authoritatively, 'Let us commit ourselves, and those we love, and all those in danger to the Lord. Then I suggest we go to bed.'

He opened the Bible with the same deliberate hands that I had watched since childhood, thinner now, and more fragile, but still firm. 'I will both lay me down in peace, and sleep: for thou, Lord, only makest me dwell in safety.'

The noise outside grew ever more deafening. Inside, the steady voice read the comforting words, and then there was silence. We sat huddled under the one rather dim light. Now as I listened to the tempest of sound echoing over the hills and along the valley to the west of us, I felt a different person, changed for the time from the girl who longed for gaiety, excitement and laughter. Faced with reality I knew I wanted a rock-like belief which could not be shaken by life's storms and tragedies; I wanted that calmness and certain hope which I saw so vividly in my father's life. This time the Bible words spoke across the centuries to me, as they had so often spoken to those who would hear them in times of violence and danger.

Slowly I climbed the stairs to my attic bedroom, listening

L

to the perpetual uncanny sound as the letter-box still rattled and trembled in tune with the shaken earth.

As I lay down a sudden screaming noise grew swiftly louder and more intense. I stiffened and almost immediately a diabolical whistling bomb, its sound intended to sap our morale, exploded nearby. The house shuddered. I buried my head in the pillow. Morning seemed an eternity away. For many it would never come, and one was sick at heart.

16

THE WEDDING

ONE day early in 1942, Tom travelled from Hove where he was a naval officer cadet, and shocked my mother by announcing that he had a fortnight's leave in three weeks time, and he thought we had better take the opportunity, and get married. 'How shall I ever be ready in time?' she said despairingly. But our minds were made up. I was always ready for adventure and risk; although we had very little money saved up, we were quite prepared to take life with both hands and walk out into the future. Who knew how long it would last? The days could hardly be more uncertain.

My father, surprisingly, understood this, and gave us his blessing. Indeed he was so fond of Tom and delighted that he was going to marry his often troublesome daughter, that I felt his pleasure was almost uncomplimentary to me. It was even a little annoying that Tom was so suitable in every way. It might almost have been a *marriage arrangée* for my father's benefit. I was far from sure if I would measure up to the required standard, and certainly at that time felt no need to consider whether I would fully return to 'the Meeting' when I was married.

Tom was happy to go to any church or chapel when he was away from home, yet he still held a steady allegiance to the little group among whom he had been brought up. 'Well, for one thing they really do worship in the way we believe those early Christians did in the New Testament', he said.

Then the vexed question of the actual wedding arose. Suddenly I knew that I deeply wanted to be married in the Parish Church where I lived. The young Vicar, a charming, dedicated man had, strangely enough, been a friend of Tom's in childhood days.

Perhaps it was a sign of a superficial character in some way, but the outward setting had always greatly influenced me. A building could be gracious or uninspiring. The 'feel' of it lay in its appearance and atmosphere. To me, the thought of a church wedding seemed beautiful and desirable. One's spirit would soar with the nobility of the architecture, leap with the rolling organ music, turn to God in the place where generations had worshipped over the long years. I told Tom. 'Well, that's alright', he said. 'I don't mind where it is, as long as the ceremony takes place.'

Together we spoke to my father. It was as if his joy in our wedding was suddenly extinguished. It appeared I had given him a mortal wound. 'You do not want to be among those who have loved and prayed for you all these years?' he said. 'You want to turn your back on the place where you belong, and on all those who want to join with you on that day?'

'Well, I can't ask any of my friends. They would find it so strange, and I would love the beautiful setting and the music.' My disappointment was bitter. I could not even have my own wedding, it seemed. This, too, was to be my father's choice, for even in my anger, I felt I could not hurt him any more.

I gave way, and from that moment the actual ceremony ceased to have any interest for me. My father, apparently jubilant again at my capitulation, took a personal and profound interest in the details. He arranged that two of the meeting elders should conduct the service. As there was no Minister, this was quite customary. He insisted that words should be inserted in the long service so that he might give me away. This was not usually done in Meeting weddings. 'In a way it will be the happiest day of my life', he said.

'Hardly a compliment to me!' I remarked drily, at which he laughed.

I was now teaching in a boys' grammar school in Bath. Each day after school had ended, I made hurried shopping expeditions, and with clothing coupons begged, borrowed and gathered from relatives and friends, I managed to scrape together enough for a simple wedding dress that would be suitable to wear afterwards, and a few new things for our honeymoon.

I arrived home one day to hear that the kind elderly wife of one of the elders, who was to officiate at our wedding, had arranged with my parents that part of her wedding gift to me would be the decoration of the meeting hall. I realised that she knew I had wanted a beautiful church wedding, and, rather touchingly, now wanted to do all she could to make the plain hall more pleasant and festive. 'Well, it's very kind of her', I said. But no amount of decoration could really make the large hall beautiful, I felt. I seemed to be standing outside the preparations, almost as if I was watching the plans for someone else's marriage. All I cared now was that we should get through the ordeal of the day itself.

I told no one except the Headmaster of the school where I was working, that I would like to get married, and he gave me a fortnight's leave of absence. The staffroom was a pleasant one; there were twenty-five men, and five women who had replaced the young men joining the forces. Often there was a great deal of teasing and chaffing. Somehow the news of the wedding leaked out.

'Why haven't you invited us?' the men said.

'It's very quiet and we don't want a fuss', I answered, but I did not tell them the real reason.

One morning I walked into my Upper V English Class, and the whole form of boys stood up and sang 'Every nice girl loves a sailor!' Then they sat down beaming rather foolishly.

'That *was* nice!' I said, overcome with laughter.

I was summoned to a special meeting of the House to which I was attached, when the Housemaster, after a charming little speech, presented me with a splendid edition of *The Oxford Companion to Music*, beautifully inscribed with my name and 'the best wishes of the boys of Dancy's House'. I was very touched.

At last the day before the wedding arrived, and with it the chilling news that the German battleships Scharnhörst and Gneisenau had escaped into the English Channel. Now fear seized me as I wondered if Tom's leave would be stopped. Perhaps there will be no wedding, I thought. The day seemed endless. At school the men were particularly kind, with I believe, a real perception of my feelings.

'We tease her enough most days. We'll let her off to-day', they said. I smiled gratefully. The hours crawled by.

Eventually I finished my last class, said a hasty goodbye to the other women on the staff who had a lovely present for me. All the staff were uniting to take my classes, and I was truly grateful to them. I ran for the bus that would take me to the station in time to meet Tom's train. The wait was dreadful.

At last the train puffed and hissed round the curve leading into the station, the doors burst open, and the platform was flooded with men from the services. It seemed eternity before I saw the tall figure of a young naval officer, no longer a cadet, looking calm, happy and reassuring, coming towards me. Quite suddenly I did not mind where or how I was married. Tom had come and everything would be alright.

Later that evening we went back to the station to meet his father who was making the long journey from the North to be at the wedding. When the train arrived, we saw a tall tired, elderly figure, resplendent in full military uniform, descend from the train.

'Oh dear!' said Tom. 'Why hasn't he come in ordinary clothes?'

In fact, Tom's father had held the rank of Major from the first World War, and his days in the army in India from 1916–1920 had been very happy ones for him. Now he was in charge of the Home Guard in the country area where he lived.

'Please don't say anything', I said. 'I think he looks splendid', I added, gazing at the red tabs and smart trench coat. As far as I was concerned, the presence of 'The Brigadier' at the wedding—as everyone called him—added a real lustre to the day, and he charmed everyone with his distinguished looks and old-world courtesy.

The day really came. It was intensely cold. My one bridesmaid arrived at the house. She was a girl of great character, who had nursed on the Labrador in the famous Mission founded by that now famous and valiant doctor, Sir Wilfred Grenfell. She was a daughter of one of the 'elder brethren' who was to conduct the Service. High-spirited, yet loyal to her family, she was one of the only friends I wanted with me, because she belonged to the same background as I. Sadly, I had not invited any of my special school or college friends, or any of the wonderful people I had grown to love in the North. I may have underestimated their affection, but I felt they would not sympathise with the service, and would find it very strange. Let those who come be able to enjoy this wedding, I thought, and at least understand the sincerity of those who conduct it.

I longed that the Presbyterian minister and his wife who had been almost like second parents to me in the North should be there, but I was afraid it would seem a strange ceremony compared to that in their Church, another place where, indeed, I could have wished the wedding service to be. I wrote to tell them I was getting married very quietly, and I have kept their letters until this day. The Minister wrote:

'This is very thrilling and delightful news. Thank you so much for writing to tell us. First of all, I am glad that you are going to be married at once. I feel sure that you are going to be very happy even though at first you won't have the normal kind of married life. And in these days when so many are sad it is good to know of some who are really happy . . .

I did like your man. He looked as though he would take care of you! I'm sorry to think of the coming separation. It will be hard on you both. May it soon come to an end.

And may the good Lord bless and keep you both when you are together and when you are separated: and may all the varied experiences of the coming days deepen your love for one another and enrich your faith in God . . .'

Dear, kind friends. If only I had been less reserved about my home, I know they would have helped me to clear my thoughts, and would have been so understanding.

Win, my bridesmaid, calmed me that morning, and together we laughed.

'This will be the Meeting wedding of the century', she said jokingly.

'Why? What do you mean?' I asked.

'Well, you'll see.' As I climbed into the taxi with my father beaming happily, and looking distinguished in morning dress and top hat, I felt as if I was about to undergo a severe ordeal.

When we arrived in the drab back street, typical of the location of many Plymouth Brethren meeting halls in those days, I was astounded to see a bright red carpet stretching to the pavement edge. I guessed now what Win had meant. The usual Brethren wedding ceremony took place, in those days, in an undecorated setting of bare simplicity.

'I should think this has never occurred before', she said, as we gazed at the carpet, fascinated.

When I walked slowly into the hall with my father, a gifted friend was playing the large harmonium—permissible on Sunday evenings in gospel meetings—with skill and expertise, and, quite surprisingly, the strains of *Here comes the Bride* echoed round the building. I saw to my surprise that very many friends of my parents had come, and even various 'worldly' relatives, their kindly faces smiling their good will. More astonishing was a forest of palm trees that appeared to have grown overnight, and the small platform was most lavishly shrouded in foliage and flowers. From amongst the greenery there gazed down upon us the two elder Brethren who were to conduct the service.

'They've tried to give me their very best', I thought with gratitude. But they could not understand that all I wanted was freedom of choice.

However, when I saw Tom standing safely there, with the young Vicar beside him in dog collar acting as best man—a unique situation in a 'Brethren' wedding—I felt I could face anything, and I experienced a wave of gratitude in my mind to those who had come to wish us well.

Together we listened intently to the long and demanding service, where the bride and groom make their promises at some length in wording not unlike the Anglican service. We listened to the talk which was deeply spiritual and earnestly given. One part I still recollect: 'It is not in the house but in the field that the wedded pair really come to know each other. It is in the open field that the bond which binds them is tempered, by the heat and cold in the open field of this world's sins and sorrows, its animosities and fears.' None knew better than the truly dedicated among the Brethren what the animosity of the world meant. None were more prepared to face it calmly and quietly.

At the moment of putting on the ring there was a hitch. It seemed too small! Tom had a fearful and prolonged struggle to get it on. A faint smile passed over his face which was unusually pale. Indeed I had been disturbed by this at the moment when he was asked if he would take this woman as his lawful wedded wife. The silence was so long before he replied that it suddenly occurred to me to wonder if he now wisely repented of the whole thing, or was feeling faint. Greatly alarmed, I nudged him gently, and at last he made the response.

'What on earth was the matter?' I asked him afterwards. 'Where you wanting to change your mind?'

'Don't be silly,' he said. 'I was sure the question had been wrongly asked, and I was just considering how to answer it properly!' I might have known that someone so 'unflappable' would not take fright at this stage.

The singing of the twenty-third metrical psalm to the Scottish tune Crimond finished the service, and was to me the most significant part:

'Yea, though I walk in death's dark vale,
    Yet will I fear none ill:
For thou art with me: and thy rod
    And staff me comfort still.'

It looked as if we might need those words of comfort before very long had passed, if the war continued to develop in severity.

At last it was all over. I knew as we walked down the aisle together and looked at the loving faces around us that we were surrounded by the genuine affection of people who really cared for us.

'Why am I not content to stay here and really to belong?'
I wondered, for 'belonging' somewhere had always seemed
so important, and for me unattainable. For a moment the
arguments raced quickly to and fro in my mind even then,
as they so often had.

'If you stay, it might be a complete withdrawal from the
real world. A tiny safe cosmos, secret, enclosed, cosy even.
If you believe in the Christian Faith you know well that it is
out in the world among the hopeless and the despairing that
so often God is to be found.'

'But the doctrines of the Christian Faith are kept here in
their early purity.'

'It may well be that having the Spirit of Christ is even
more important than soundness of doctrine.'

'Your father will break his heart if you leave. The others
have all left.'

'I know. How well I know. But is it to be my mission in life
to be dutiful to him?'

As I left the hall with Tom, the arguments had all faded
away, for I felt somehow, sometime, he would know the
right answers. Meanwhile it was obvious that my father was
greatly enjoying the day.

'I wondered if we would ever be married when the ring
wouldn't go on!' I said, as we travelled in a taxi to my home,
where the relatives were to be entertained at a small lunch
party.

'You need not have worried', Tom answered, 'I was determined to get it on somehow, and was quite prepared to
draw blood if necessary!'

We laughed. The ordeal was really over, and now I was
ready to begin a new life.

17

'YET WILL I FEAR NO ILL'

Our honeymoon began in a tiny hotel in Polperro in Cornwall, which had fascinating bull's eye windows in the roof, and here we could see the sea-gulls stepping to and fro across the thick glass and peering in at us. It was bitterly cold. In the evenings, the four guests, an elderly couple and ourselves, huddled around the inadequate fire in the long low sitting room, with its dark overhanging beams. The old lady and her husband wrapped themselves in rugs, and we shivered.

Here Tom, ever practical and mindful of his legal duties, produced his new will, and asked the old couple to witness it. A macabre honeymoon task, I thought, emphasising how uncertain were the times in which we lived. On the fifth day of our stay a telegram came recalling Tom, instructing him to proceed to Portsmouth for further gunnery training at Whale Island. Our honeymoon was untimely over.

I decided to spend the rest of my fortnight's leave of absence near him. We arrived in Portsmouth late at night after a long slow journey.

'We want to go to some quiet hotel', Tom told the taxi-driver in the station yard.

'Hotel!' the man laughed bitterly. 'There's not a single hotel left standing in Portsmouth, and there are only two in Southsea left. But they are always full. You'll never get in.'

'Well, we must stay somewhere', we said.

Rather unwillingly the taxi-driver said he would try the two in Southsea although it would be useless. The first was a tall Victorian house, the walls cracked severely from top to bottom. There were no rooms available. We went to the second and last choice and walked into a larger more solid hotel on the sea front surrounded by barbed wire. It seemed to be full of Royal Navy personnel passing to and fro in the hall. Feeling a little foolish, Tom approached the brisk receptionist.

'Well, if you two aren't the luckiest people!' she said. 'I've just had a cancellation of a double room half an hour ago. Something that just never happens.' Then she gazed rather piercingly at us over her horn-rimmed spectacles. 'It's just twin beds though!' she added warningly. Even the twin beds were no deterrent in such circumstances.

I spent the long days wandering round what was left of Portsmouth and Southsea after the massive air raids. I talked to many other young wives waiting for their husbands' ships to come and go; others who simply lived there, as their homes were destroyed and it was as good a place to be as any if you had no home, and your husband could join you there from time to time. Some had had no news for a long time; they spent endless hours knitting—and waiting. All in all it was a depressing place and I counted the hours until evening came when Tom would come back.

At the end of two weeks we parted again. Tom went north to Queensferry to begin his Minesweeper Training and I returned to my job until the end of term.

.   .   .   .   .

My plans were uncertain. Tom and I decided that as long as it was possible I would 'follow the Fleet'. We lived briefly in Edinburgh, and Newcastle, and then Tom was posted as 2nd lieutenant to his first ship, *H.M.S. Strephon*, a minesweeper, based on Tilbury docks.

It was difficult to find anywhere to live. At last Tom found lodgings across the Thames at Gravesend in a tiny house with cherry trees at the front gate. Here he joined me when he

could, crossing from Tilbury to Gravesend on the ferry. I got
a job in Greenhithe, teaching in a Secondary School half
blown away by a bomb, the end of its buildings a jagged
wreck. The children were very poor, their clothes ragged and
their i.q. was not high. They had obviously not settled in the
evacuation areas, because they had returned to their homes,
many of which were subsequently destroyed. But their cheerfulness and resilience were wonderful. They lived as if nothing
was wrong, and their chief love was rabbits. These they kept
and cared for devotedly at the school. One guessed that the
children were fed inadequately at home, but excellent hot
dinners were brought round by large mobile canteens each
day, and this kept them tough and quite healthy.

Each evening I took the bus back from work, eagerly
hoping that Tom might be waiting at the lodgings where we
lived. Mrs. Neill, who owned the house, was a widow, a tiny,
pale, delicate-featured, little woman. She gave us plain, very
badly cooked food but much affection. She also had a
wealth of earthy information to impart. She had been
married twice. Her first husband had been a drunkard who
ill-treated her. But 'Mr. Neill' was a 'gentleman'. 'He was
wonderfully kind to me, dearie, but I looked after him and
loved him until he died. Ever so gentle he was! Do you know
I was that nervous when I married him, I didn't know what
to do. So I kept my corsets on in bed! And he never touched
me, love. Yes, Mr. Neill was a real gentleman.' A furtive tear
would creep down.

Dear Mrs. Neill. We suffered together. Her idolised son
was in the Merchant Navy, on a tanker. Sometimes it was
overdue and she was overcome with worry. Then, one
evening Tom did not come home when he was due. Her
terror was real and sincere. I cycled down to the ferry, and
there when the gentle summer evening light was bathing the
river in a soft sunset glow, I stood and watched for a sight of

the balloons that flew from the minesweeping trawlers as they sailed in and out of port. One could often see a pale grey dot in the sky moving very slowly, as the ship made its way up the river; it would grow larger and clearer, and then another and another would emerge from the mist of distance, for the minesweepers came and went in a group of four.

I waited and watched for a time that seemed endless. I saw large merchant vessels come limping into port with battered hulls, signs of having suffered in an air attack. I saw the golden sky dim to soft grey and the first star appear; a little chill breeze sprang up and gently ruffled the water, and three dark shapes slowly, wearily, almost, slid up the river and berthed. The minesweepers were in, but *H.M.S. Strephon* was not with them. I waited until darkness shrouded the river, and sick at heart I pushed my bicycle home.

Mrs. Neill was at the front gate, a ghost in the shadows, waiting silently. Wearily I went in.

'What news, dear?'

'Tom's ship hasn't come, Mrs. Neill. The others are in.'

'God help us, dear. He'll come.' She flung her arms around me, but I was numb with fear.

It was not until the next morning after a restless tortured night that the phone went.

'Hallo, dear. Everything o.k.?'

'Oh! Tom. I thought . . .'

'Well that was silly of you wasn't it? All's well, mission accomplished, and I'll be up early to-day.'

'Mrs. Neill, Tom's home!'

'Thank God, thank God. I haven't slept a wink. I'll make a good hot cup of tea!'

Mrs. Neill had a large dark brown heavy metal table in her sitting-room. This was a Morrison table shelter and in the event of air raids the family would creep under it. Whole families were often saved by these when houses collapsed in the Blitz, and they were found unscathed in the shelter.

The first time it was used, after we arrived, was during a heavy raid some miles away. The whole procedure had an unreal quality. Tom was at sea that night, and Mrs. Neill, more wraith-like than ever in her white nightdress, summoned me from bed just as the siren was howling its warning. A loud and urgent tapping on the back door heralded the arrival of an elderly widowed neighbour, also in a white nightdress, with her coat on top, carrying cushions, her Bible, and false teeth in a glass. An eldritch figure, she had wild white hair, not particularly clean, which stuck out in spikes all over her head.

'Well, dearie, what ho! Here we are', she announced cheerfully, as if an unexpected party had been arranged for midnight.

'Me rheumatics are cruel', she added merrily as she knelt down creakily to crawl into the shelter first. It took some. time for her to arrange her stiff limbs on the few cushions and straighten herself out.

Then little Mrs. Neill crept in, a tiny figure uttering whispered comments of encouragement and exhortation. She lay alongside her neighbour, and beckoned with a pale little hand to me to enter.

'Cheerio, love. In you come.'

So I crept in last and stretched myself beside her, and there we lay, three oddly assorted souls, waiting . . .

Presently a distant humming noise could be heard.

'E's coming, dear', said the neighbour. 'Proper punctual, the devil. Mark my words, 'e'll come to a bad end.'

The noise grew more steady and insistent, an uneven drumming. Now and again there was a sound of anti-aircraft fire. Then suddenly the distant earth shook, and a tremor passed through the floor beneath us.

'Dear God, save us', Mrs. Neill whispered.

'Well dear, they say you're alright if your number isn't on the bomb', the neighbour talked on garrulously. 'And of course if it is, you've 'ad it, 'aven't you? Still, I believe in angels, oh! yes. They was seen at Mons, wasn't they? Well, then. We're surrounded by them now, I don't doubt.' The old voice chattered on.

Outside the noise grew deafeningly loud. Mrs. Neill trembled and began clasping and unclasping her hands. I put my fingers in my ears. It was the gesture of the child who was too frightened to hear about the Second Coming. And so we lay in the total darkness of the tiny room, enclosed in a metal prison, each with her private thoughts and fears, while up above us German aircraft passed continuously and relentlessly across the moonlit sky.

Some weeks later Tom was again at sea. His ship was on a special mission towing barges up and down the Channel, presumably to try and persuade the Germans that preparations for the second Front were in progress. All work in the Channel was dangerous. At this time London was quiet, but heavy air raids were occurring spasmodically in provincial cities. I had always regarded Bath as a comparatively safe area. On this particular morning I received a telegram from my parents, saying, briefly, 'Safe and well.'

'What can have happened?' I said to Mrs. Neill. 'Surely there have been no raids there.'

That night I listened to the news and was astonished to hear that our city had endured a very heavy raid during the night. No details were given. As I had the telegram, I thought that everything must be well at home. The next day when I got back from school I found a strangely dirty-looking letter from my mother:

Darling,
    Our home was blitzed to the ground last night, but we

M

are safe and well. After a wonderful escape we came to the hospital, so that a small wound on Daddy's head can be treated.

Love from
Mother.

Unbelievingly, I read it over several times. Very slowly, incredulously almost, I took in the meaning, and gradually the horror of it flowed over me. What had they endured there alone, what would they do with no home, no possessions, very little money, and only their courage to sustain them? Then and there I put my head down on the back of the dingy settee and at long last the tears I could so often have shed for them over the years, came fast and free. It was there that Mrs. Neill found me. I pushed the letter into her hand, and together we sat there, she stroking my hand, gently, while her own tears of sympathy fell untidily down her pale cheeks.

The next evening another very heavy raid on Bath was announced over the radio. Tom eventually came home and we went to the police to see if they could get any news of my parents. But it appeared no phone contact could be made with the stricken city, which was virtually cut off, as no trains could reach it either, owing to destruction on the railway. We could only wait, and I wondered if they were still alive. Another day went and there was still no news. Tom's understanding Commanding Officer then gave him compassionate leave for five days so that we might go and see if we could find them.

At Paddington Station we found we could take a train to a little village some miles outside the city, and from there buses were waiting to complete the journey. Eventually we got out at a tiny country station in the warm sunshine of an early summer day, and got into the bus which slowly moved off in the direction of the city centre. Near the outskirts we could see the odd gap in the long rows of tall stone houses, could see clouds of dust in the distance and became aware of a peculiar acrid smell of burning in the air. Then as we made our way right into the city, the streets were suddenly full of broken glass, shattered buildings, great piles of rubble, and some streets seemed to have vanished in a chaos of earth and stones. The streets were crowded with troops, A.R.P. workers and firemen, while demolition squads worked tirelessly to bring down the unsafe tottering walls which from time to time swayed and crashed to the ground in clouds of dust. The men were covered with a thin grey film, and many worked stripped to the waist.

Hardly knowing where to begin when we left the bus, we looked around at the many notices displayed in many places. We read that all water must be boiled because of danger of typhoid fever from the burst and contaminated water mains. We read directions to find the various reception centres, enquiry offices, Red Cross headquarters and the many mobile canteens carrying tea, hot soup, bread and sandwiches for those who had no cooking facilities, or no homes. Lastly we saw, starkly hanging on the various notice boards, the lists. I could not speak, for here were the lists of the dead, many long rows of names, and the places where they had been found.

'Look and see', I said to Tom in a whisper.

It took a long time to read them, and now and again came a name one knew. But not my parents.

We had a feeling that they would have gone to some kind friends just outside the city itself. It was they who had decorated the meeting hall for our wedding. We wandered from phone box to phone box. All were damaged or out of order. But, near the Guildhall, one box was at last found which worked.

'You see please', I said to Tom.

I watched his face through the glass. If the news was bad, I was better outside, so as not to upset him. The wait seemed very long. Then, suddenly, I saw a delighted smile on his face and I knew he had found them. He came outside with the good news that they were there and a bus was still running to that part of the outskirts of Bath. For once I was silent with the great relief, but as the bus slowly climbed the hill towards our destination and I saw the wreckage around us, I knew there would be many whose day would not end in happiness nor in any reunion.

We climbed out of the bus at last, and there we saw them, waiting for us. My mother was dressed in most peculiar and ill-fitting clothes, and on her head was perched a little green hat in which she looked undignified and faintly ridiculous. Comedy had mercifully intervened to break the tension.

'Oh! Mum, you look incredible!' I said, and we all burst out laughing.

'Fancy laughing at my nice new clothes!' she said gaily. I learned later she had been in her night clothes when the house collapsed and now had nothing of her own.

I gazed at my father. What effect had this nightmare had on him? Then I saw his silvery white hair had turned to a dark grey-black colour, and there was a wound dressing on his head.

'Your hair, Dad. What's happened?' He laughed.

'Don't you think I look much younger?' he said. 'It's just the effects of the blast, and most annoyingly I'm not allowed to wash my head properly because of this little wound.'

For five days Tom and I searched in the rubble and the remains of the back of the house, part of which still stood, in a dangerous condition, for any possessions, and any clothes that could be found. The entire front half of the house had been pulverised, and everything I possessed had gone as well, for I had only been living with two small suitcases. But my father's dressing-room remained, buried in rubble and plaster.

'What do you want us to look for?' I asked him.

'Well, dear, I really do miss my little Greek New Testament so much', he said. He had no thoughts for all his treasures gathered over the years, his wonderful library of medical books.

'I suppose a few clothes would be useful', he added as an afterthought,—'if there are any.'

Later, we learned that they had been together under the stairs when the raid started; and when early on the front of the house was demolished when the bomb fell, barely fifteen feet away from them, they found themselves half buried under the wreckage and the remains of the stair case, gazing out at the night sky and at the trees in the road all ablaze like torches.

'Were you dreadfully scared, Dad?' His answer was serene.

'It was really wonderful how calm we were kept. I held mother's hand and we said the twenty-third psalm together, and we felt we were not alone.'

By a miracle they had not been killed by the blast as they should have been, and they had managed somehow to free themselves and climb out over towering mounds of stone and rubble. They helped to rescue an old lady of ninety-three from the next house, and asked some passing men to carry her with them to the hospital nearby, and then had set off on a slow weary pilgrimage, my father bleeding from the wound in his head. A very low flying German aircraft machine-gunned this little helpless group as, in the bright moonlight, they stumbled along.

For two years my parents lived in an attic in the home of their kind friends. Many thousands of houses had been destroyed in the two raids. They were quite unable to get together a new home, and accommodation to let was almost unobtainable. Day after day my mother trudged from house to house, trying to find somewhere to live, but often others had got there first. She, I think, never fully recovered from the shock; but during this time I never once heard my father complain. He appeared quiet and calm, as if he was grateful for anything that the Lord might provide, and he was unmoved by misfortune and deprivation.

18

THE MESSAGE

THESE were the difficult years, sometimes sad, often lonely. The one thing that carried us through many situations was a sense of humour, and at a deeper level we clung to the belief that there was a purpose in life, even if at this time it seemed particularly hidden. At this time we were like 'strangers and pilgrims', moving constantly from place to place. I continued to move from port to port following the ship, for now I had no home to go to, even if it had seemed desirable.

Because there was never time to settle anywhere, I did not probe too deeply into the problem of where I belonged, whether in The Brethren or elsewhere. The important thing seemed to be that, come wind, come weather, Tom's faith was firm and deep, and I looked to him for inspiration. It did not seem to matter, then, that we had no fixed and final allegiance to any one branch of the Christian Church, for we were happy to go anywhere, depending on where we found ourselves. There was one thing that remained constant in my mind. That was a sure conviction that the Christian faith could be a tremendous force and dynamic in one's life. I did not always agree with my father's Puritan outlook, but I knew that his faith was so real, so powerful, that it put that of many so-called Christians to shame. Somewhere I wanted to find the reconciling link between a full and free life, as I felt it should be lived—without limiting rules and regulations imposed from outside—and a faith that meant everything. Sometimes, in frustration, I felt angry because I could not find what I wanted. I went to many churches which seemed lifeless, I looked in vain for that dynamic life I believed existed in true Christianity; and often in anger I turned back to the simple Brethren meeting where the faith meant everything to its members. Yet there I felt an outsider so often, because I could not subscribe to the limited way of life that many of them lived, to their withdrawal from much that was beautiful and significant in the world: great literature, art, drama, music, and mixing freely and happily with those of different views and beliefs. There were, of course, exceptions to this, but the doctrine of 'separation' still held true for the majority. Of all the churches I visited, I felt most at home in the Church of England, where it was often apparent that there was a real effort to make faith relevant to the modern world.

I think that all the time I was searching for something almost without knowing what I wanted or expected to find. Whatever it was, it would have to be the real thing, and I was not sure if I would ever be satisfied.

At this time Tom was made a lieutenant and put in command of *H.M.S. Strephon*. The ship was sent north to the icy waters outside Aberdeen where she was based for three years. Here the weather was the dreaded enemy. Bitter cold and violent storms in winter increased the danger for the trawlers, as steadily and regularly they moved north and south to keep the sea lanes open.

One night when *Strephon* had been on a special mission, sailing towards Norway, a tempest of wind blew up, and the little ship was blown off course on her return journey. After cryptic messages were exchanged with the home base it appeared she had been blown into the middle of the minefield. Her chances of escaping were small indeed. So great was her danger, that a message suddenly came through to her that every light on the coast was to be turned on, to help her regain her correct position. This in a time of strict blackout was unheard of. Somehow the hours passed and she eventually emerged unscathed after a very tense experience.

We experienced an endless variety of lodgings, guest houses and rooms in Aberdeen. Somehow they never seemed to last, for a strange variety of reasons. Our residence in a solid old-fashioned house, where we rented two rather beautiful rooms full of splendid antique furniture, and 'did' for ourselves, sharing the kitchen, came to an abrupt end when I developed measles. After supervising with some delight my departure,—prone on a stretcher, swathed in red blankets, to the fever hospital—the owner of the house, terrified at the displeasing prospect of nursing me, danced a sort of jig on the pavement, with relief, as the hearse-like black ambulance careered away to the dockside area where the hospital was situated. Thereafter she decided my strength would be too enfeebled to polish the mahogany furniture properly. She told Tom to find other accommodation.

After weary searching, he at last discovered a somewhat down-at-heels guest house. We took up residence amid a variety of inmates. There was a dignified, sprightly, elderly lady of immense courage and charm, who was, as would then have been described, 'in reduced circumstances'. With a back like a ramrod, and twinkling frosty blue eyes, she gave the guest house a certain aura of respectability. This was somewhat marred by the perpetually drunken but pleasant army officer and his rather sad wife, who many a night went to bring him home from various pubs. His unsteady ascent of the stairs became part of the nightly ritual of the house. Utterly invisible, in another room, lay an elderly invalid, who had a pleasant nurse attendant living with her. Strangest of all, perhaps, was the Anthroposophist. This amiable middle-aged lady of indeterminate appearance, who had fled from the bombing of the south coast of England, was a devotee of the Thought and Works of Rudolf Steiner. Each evening in winter—and it was cold in the north of Scotland, a sort of vicious penetrating knife-like cold—she sat wrapped in the double thickness of a large rug in front of the minute sitting-room fire, with vast tomes enshrining the wisdom of her prophet on her knee. From her I learned a number of incredible facts, among them that tomatoes planted by the light of the full moon, always supposing you were hardy enough to attempt this, grew to at least twice the normal size; and that mentally retarded children, if awakened to the strains of the violin each day, made spectacular progress. But even the enlightenment all this afforded her, did not ease the violent pangs of hunger we all shared. The food was almost non-existent. An evening meal of a kipper and one slice of bread left us like ravening wolves. Only Miss Hawk, the elderly lady, endured, with incredible cheerfulness and acceptance.

However, our home here came to an abrupt end when a heavy air raid of great intensity, nearly blew the house and all of us to the next world. In fact we miraculously escaped harm. Although the house seemed to be falling about our ears, it was the massive granite church immediately opposite that chiefly suffered. In one violent explosion, half of it disappeared entirely, leaving a wooden cross unharmed, fixed on a beam jutting out from a shattered wall, outlined in the moonlight,—a symbol I thought, that certain things were indestructible.

Eventually we were fortunate indeed, we felt, to find two tiny attic rooms to rent at a reasonable figure in Aberdeen itself. Here, too, life was odd, sometimes even amusing. The house was owned by a gigantic figure of a man, a Dane, and his musical wife. We had a tiny boxroom, hardly big enough to turn round in, which we used as a kitchen. In it was a minute sink. We were warned not to throw rubbish down this. Carefully I had to collect everything in a bucket and descend two flights of stairs to pour any dirty water away in the bathroom, and rubbish had to be carried a further two flights to the ground floor. It was a tedious business.

We tried to keep this rule but now and then a few errant tea-leaves and bits of rubbish would float away down the sink. I wondered why this rule was imposed on us, and felt that if I was careful I need not worry too much. One day the Dane shouted loudly to Tom to descend with me and visit his bedroom. Somewhat surprised, we entered the room, its windows always hermetically sealed, and gazed at the immense double bed, beside which was the wash basin. A strange smell pervaded the stuffy atmosphere. 'Kindly watch me', he said very stiffly. 'First one of you turn on the tap in your sink upstairs, and then descend to this room.' His commands were somewhat brusquely expressed. Tom ran up and turned on the tap in our kitchenette and ran down. Soon a rather sinister gurgling sound was heard above, and then as we watched fascinated, we saw a fountain of dirty water shoot up into the air in the bedside basin and spray dirty water, filled with tea-leaves, crumbs and tiny bits of rubbish in a splendid powerful cascade all over the pillow of the double bed. Suddenly I felt I could not remain solemn. My face slipped. The thought of the nightly scene as this couple lay in bed, while we inadvertently let the water run out of the sink above, was too much! Shamefacedly we crept upstairs, almost unable to control our laughter, and wondering what use a sink was if it could not be used.

Meanwhile I had been teaching in a girl's High School for a time, and this I quite enjoyed, until I had to give it up as we were expecting our first baby. We were still in the tiny flat, and now I found the long days interminable and would kneel at the attic window gazing out over the rooftops of the city, looking towards the distant sea and watching for the ships' balloons. The year was 1944, and we believed the Second Front was imminent. Tom and I knew he might suddenly be sent away with little or no notice. Perhaps it was an inner anxiety about this but I became very ill almost without realising it. My head felt as if it was strangely gripped by iron bands. I was conscious that there was no one to help me, and it became increasingly difficult to struggle down the stairs to the nearby shop for food. Tom was away at sea for several nights, and I lay alone in the flat thinking that I should have been warned how unpleasant having a baby seemed to be.

At last came the day for the visit to the skilled gynaecologist whose patient I was. To my dismay I was rushed into a nursing home almost immediately, although the baby was not due for a month. As I lay there feeling very weak, alone in a small ward, the realisation suddenly came that perhaps this was the end. I did not feel ready to face this. As usual, my old fears surged back to mock and torture. I am like Mr. Ready-to-Halt in *Pilgrim's Progress* I thought sadly, and the words of Christiana to him came to mind: 'Thy travel hither hath been with difficulty.' Somehow faith had always been difficult for me, greatly as I desired it. I remembered that a message had been brought to Mr. Ready-to-Halt when it was time for him to cross the river at the end of his life; and for me there was a deep and significant meaning in the words:

'I am come to thee in the name of Him whom thou hast loved and followed, though upon crutches' . . . So often I, too, travelled 'on crutches'.

With this thought, I turned in a moment of fear and desperation to the only source of comfort. It was not much of a prayer for I felt like a drowning soul: 'Please help me.' It was the cry that has been sent out in weakness and fear all down the centuries, but as so often before, something happened. I picked up my small Bible that I carried with me, and barely realising what I did, I opened it and read exactly

what was before me. It was Psalm 27, and somehow the
words were speaking to me in a new and living way, and
presently I stopped at certain words, for they almost seemed
to be illuminated: 'I had fainted, unless I had believed to see
the goodness of the Lord in the land of the living' . . . 'The
land of the living!' I thought, and suddenly it seemed as if a
new hope flowed into me.

Tom came off the ship to see me later. He had been with
the doctor.

'You are going to have an operation and have the baby
to-night', he said. He chatted quietly and with an obvious
effort to be cheerful. Just before he went he said, 'I'm allowed
to stay here to-night. Would you like me to read a piece from
the Bible before I go downstairs?' 'Yes, please,' I said, and
waited half in a dream, until after a pause he said, 'Well, I
think I'll read Psalm 27.'

Suddenly I smiled. At long last, I felt as if a message had
been sent to me, and my spirit was helped. It had come at a
moment when I was too tired and hopeless to put up any
false barriers. At certain moments in life, it is as if the naked
soul shivers before its Maker, stripped of all illusions, mock
fantasies, false pride. I believe this is the point when one can
hear and receive, because it is, in a way, the moment of
Truth.

That night our little son was born. He was given a fifty per
cent chance of survival. As I looked at all four and a half
pounds of him, I felt a conviction that he would live.
I knew in my heart that I wanted him to grow up to be a
man of faith, because I believed that only so would he find
true happiness.

By a strange coincidence, in the room next to mine at this
time, another little boy was born, the posthumous son of a
brilliant father, tragically killed some months earlier in an
air crash. Orde Jonathan Wingate, son of Brigadier Orde

Wingate of Burma, lay beside David, our son, whose life for a time hung in the balance. Years before, as I have recounted, the grandparents of both these children had met in a small house in Devon, where, as was natural to them, they talked together with joy of their mutual faith.

Because of my illness, the Officer Commanding Mine-sweepers with great understanding and kindness, ordered *H.M.S. Strephon* to stay in Northern waters for a time, so that Tom could be near at hand. The other three trawlers went south to the Second Front. To our grief, we heard later that the minesweeper replacing *Strephon*, which was one of the very first to approach the coast of France on D day, was blown up by a mine as she approached her destination, and sank with the loss of all hands.

19

FAREWELL

NOWADAYS when many young people get married, they have so many material possessions—a house, furniture, carpets, modern equipment, perfect decorations—that I sometimes wonder if they have left all element of excitement and risk out of their marriage, and will become bored with their apparent good fortune.

At the end of the long war years, when the last siren had sounded, and the church bells rang out again over city and country, we were, in Biblical language, 'like them that dream'. It seemed too good to be true. When we managed to purchase, with our very modest savings, a cheap house ruined by damp, whose previous owners had forgotten to turn the water off before going on holiday in midwinter so that all the pipes burst, we were overcome with happiness. After decorating and distempering it, drying it out, and finding some very cheap furniture at auction sales and junk shops, it was home indeed. Tom had returned to his country practice as a lawyer in a small market town in the dales.

Here we attended the local Methodist Church which was thriving under a young and energetic Minister, who had just returned from being a chaplain in the forces. Although we never formally joined their fellowship, we were welcomed as part of the congregation, and invited to take communion with them, which we were glad to do.

At this time our second son was born; I was well and he was a healthy happy baby. For a time I had ceased to question anything. I was content just to be—and to know peace and security. Eventually Tom had to return to the

family practice in Newcastle, and I knew the time had come
when I must ultimately face up to the question that had
lain in my mind for so many years. For the sake of the
children we must know where we stood.

I felt I must take a last long careful look at the Plymouth
Brethren and examine their tenets. Was it possible that in this
very simple form of worship lay the truth, the heart of the
Christian faith? I believed I could never agree with their
attitude that their way was the right one to the exclusion of all
others. What gave them this seemingly arrogant sense of
certainty? Sometimes I talked it over with Tom and with a
few friends brought up like ourselves, who were also now
questioning where they stood.

The movement had started in the 1830's as a gathering
and fellowship of all who loved Christ from any and every
denomination, who wished to enjoy the fellowship of studying
the Bible together. They regarded the Scriptures as the literal
inspired Word of God, and as the final and authoritative
guide in all matters of faith and conduct. New Testament
practices, especially in the Acts and the Epistles, were regarded as showing the right and correct method of meeting
together as a church; and the members of these fellowships
or 'Assemblies', as they soon came to be called, accepted the
doctrine that all 'believers', without denominational distinc-
tions, should be free to worship together at 'the Lord's
Table'. This was regarded as a service of remembrance of
the death of our Lord, and the words, 'This do in remembrance of me' were central.

It was not long before the Assemblies began to take
precedence over the previous denominational loyalties of the
members. The movement had begun. It must be remembered
that this had come about when much of the life of the
churches was at a low ebb, and the movement had found in
itself new life and impetus.

It is always easy to be wise after the event. But it seems to me that if many of the dedicated Anglicans who joined the first groups of Brethren—strange as this now seems—had remained in their own church and had used their talents and zeal there, the result would have been of great value in a far wider sphere. They were joined by a rising tide of followers from all denominations dissatisfied with the lack of apostolic faith and teaching in their churches and chapels.

But as in all intense groups, arguments arose over the teaching of the Epistles concerning Church practice, and over the years many splits were caused, giving rise to even more exclusive small conventicles who still exist in various areas; these are still known as the various branches of the 'Exclusive Brethren', many devout and sincere, but a few finding their home in the ultimate narrowness of outlook and dreadful teaching of one tiny group, publicised in the Press a year or two ago, which scandalised all right thinking people, and brought condemnation from the Archbishop of Canterbury, among others.

The Open Brethren, among whom I was brought up, however, generally remained true to the original belief that all faithful Christians should be free to meet at the Lord's Table. With this I was in complete agreement. But where I could never join with them, was their insistence that when you joined the Brethren through the Baptism of Believers, you came out from the sects with their varied and insidious errors, and joined the Church of God. I firmly and always believed that the Church Universal consisted of all those who were committed to Christ in any and every denomination and group. I also questioned, very strongly, whether soundness of doctrine, on which they laid so much stress, was of importance in a man if he had not in his heart a profound love for humanity, so that he did not withdraw from men, but went among them in the manner of our Lord, who was

N

condemned by the Pharisees and Scribes for eating and drinking with publicans and sinners.

I agreed with them that the Bible was the inspired Word of God, although having worked at Anglo-Saxon literature at university, I knew, in a tiny measure, the problems of a translator; and a too narrow literal explanation of the Authorised Version sometimes seemed to me to confine the limitless spirit of God within their own interpretation, at least as they presented it to others. I may here be unjust, but I sometimes wondered if they were occasionally in danger of worshipping the Book rather than the Creator.

They were undoubtedly seen at their best on the mission field. Determined, intrepid, dedicated, they ventured into many lands, often pioneering where none had been before. Here the daring among them found an outlet for initiative and adventure, linked to the main task of carrying the Gospel as their Lord commanded. The large number who went overseas was higher than that of almost any other Christian group or denomination in proportion to their membership.

Their organisation was uncomplicated because almost non-existent. In a sense this was very good. The meeting was entirely and adequately supported by voluntary effort. No financial appeals were ever necessary. The expenses were low because the meeting halls were of the simplest and plainest, and always undecorated. There was no pictorial or inspirational aid for the mind. For the meditative saint this may have been salutary. For the restless sinner, the result was sometimes the opposite.

The authority in each Assembly rested in the elders, or members of the 'oversight', as they called themselves. These considered the welfare of the Church and its members, and any disagreements or moral lapses, which were very rare; or perhaps difficult questions such as who might be received into fellowship, and what Communion should be held with the various other Assemblies. Even amongst themselves, certain Assemblies were sometimes in disfavour for any rash innovation or practice. I felt that here they were often in danger of a wrong emphasis, of concentrating on non-essentials. Christendom is only weakened by such internal disagreements.

The members of the oversight were not elected but 'recognised' as holding the office by the other elders and the meeting members, because of their leading and teaching. Here there was room for abuse. Sometimes unspiritual men with a gift for talk assumed office, and obviously enjoyed their power, while genuinely spiritual men were overlooked.

Finally, certain attitudes sometimes caused unhappiness. The one weakness forbidden in Brethren Assemblies, at that time, was having doubts about any aspect of the faith revealed in Scripture and interpreted by them. I frequently wondered whether it was possible that these people, so secure and settled in outlook, really did not even suffer in their hearts the sadness and disillusionment that so often comes to ordinary men and women from time to time, who may yet long for reassurance and certainty.

It seemed to me that the most dedicated among them, like my father, lived close to their Master, seeking his guidance through prayer and Bible reading for every aspect of their lives. Their faith was steady, almost relentlessly firm, and they would point the way to Salvation with a clear-eyed assurance. Their armour was impregnable. This I admired in them. But the difficulty arose when the less imaginative and sympathetic among them could not, on this account, offer help, sympathy or any understanding to the one who honestly wanted the truth, but could not see it as they did. They were able to preach to the 'unbeliever', the 'sinner', the 'lost'. But they were in danger of ignoring and misunderstanding the real *person*, with all his human idiosyncrasies, his failures and longings, his different individual needs.

When I expressed true and sincere doubts about some part of the faith as presented by them, their answer was given in the words of Scripture. It was a diagnosis: 'Satan hath desired to have you that he may sift you as wheat. But I have prayed for you that your faith fail not.' One felt the horror of a cosmic conflict.

I therefore came to believe that the quiet concern of Christ with the *individual* and his special problems was not always adequately stressed. For he came to doubting Thomas, not with censure, but with practical immediate help: 'Reach hither thy hand'—and Thomas believed. When Peter began to sink in the waves, Christ was immediately beside him, and the gentle understanding words restored the one who was so impetuous and eager, but so prone to failure: 'O thou of little faith, wherefore didst thou doubt.' It was each time a loving personal meeting with the one who most needed him.

I realised, therefore, that it is at the moment when a man blinded by uncertainties, and failures, turns to God and holds out his hands in need, empty of all save his doubts and fears, that he is ready for the first Divine encounter, and is enabled to take the first step to a new life.

On returning to Newcastle we had returned to the meeting for a time, almost in a spirit of exploration. I believe that the hold the Brethren have over those brought up in their midst is very strong. I have heard it likened to being brought up in the Roman Catholic Church, because although so diametrically opposed in much doctrine, these two extremes are authoritarian, and definite. The mind is ceaselessly instructed in the true doctrine, the correct belief, the right attitude, and, in the Brethren, rigid behaviour patterns.

Tom now began slowly to feel that there was no freedom in the meeting to do what he believed was right. He was criticised publicly by some of the older brethren for joining with members of other denominations in various ecumenical activities. This seemed intolerable and wrong.

The more I thought it over, the more I had begun to believe that the Church of England had for long been the place where I should be. All my life I had attended Anglican services when the opportunity arose, and here I felt there was freedom to believe in and practice the truth as I saw it. And if at times the Church seemed vague rather than authoritarian in some of its pulpit pronouncements, yet it always welcomed its members not as saints but as sinners to find forgiveness and peace. The root of the Christian faith lay in its liturgy and the Biblical words of the lessons, not in the words of men who might or might not be motivated by the true spirit of God.

As I thought over all these things more calmly than I had ever been able to do in the past, it never ceased to seem tragic that men should waste their time disputing doctrinaire differences, sectarian quarrels and theological arguments, when the prime task of the Church Universal was to carry the Good News of love, compassion and redemption to the lost and the hopeless, the disreputable and the outcast, the sick and the sorrowful, and to all men who would receive it.

If heredity had any influence, I guessed I was moving steadily to the place from where my mother came. I had envied her that happy normal Vicarage life. It seemed that soon we must make a firm decision, and not least for the sake of our children. Tom, I knew, would do what he believed to be right, when the time came and his mind was made up. But still there was just one thing holding me back.

.   .   .   .   .

Although my parents found a flat to live in at long last, the war years had drained them of vitality. When one visited them there was the same delight, the same courtesy, but they were only able to live very quietly.

In time it was apparent that my father's strength was slowly ebbing away. He became bedridden, his sight failed, and it was a great grief and deprivation when he could no longer read. One Spring day I travelled south alone to see him, because constant nursing care had become essential as he was quite helpless, and he had to go into hospital in a day or two. It was distressing to see him so weak, and I sat with him, beside his bed. He had given his whole life to heal the sick, and now there was nothing that could be done for him.

For a time we talked about the children, and about life in the North, and at first he listened with the old intentness and pleasure. His mind was clear but his expression from time to time grew far away, and then he gazed thoughtfully, sadly, at me as if he knew there was very little time to say those things which he had to. Presently he said,

'At last I am nearing the end of my journey.'

'Is it weary, Dad?'

'This part is', he said with a gentle smile. He paused for a long time, and then he seemed to gather his strength and began to question me about the Brethren meeting to which we had recently been going. With a great effort he said at last, 'Are you happy there?'

'No, Dad. There is no freedom. The rules are so often of their own making. If you felt God wanted you to do something unusual and did it, they would almost certainly disapprove. Tom has been publicly criticised for some of the Christian work he does with people from many other churches—rightly—instead of just working in their tiny group.'

There was another pause, then he summoned his failing strength. 'That is so wrong', he said, and went on slowly, 'I believe the time has come when you may no longer be able to stay in "The Meeting". May God guide you where to go.' His voice was sad.

I took his hand. I knew then that I had at last been given the freedom for which I longed. I had been given it freely by the only person from whom I was willing to take it. For I realised quite suddenly and clearly in that moment, that my bondage had been, in a measure, self-imposed. I had wanted the door to freedom to be opened from the outside, by one person only.

The time for my train drew near. I got up. My father held out his hand.

'Kiss me, darling, before you go.'

It was a farewell, and I knew, also, a benediction.

I was never to hear that voice again.

20

'THE END OF THE BEGINNING'

MY mother survived my father by less than a year. Exhausted with nursing him, her health rapidly deteriorated. I think when he had gone, the mainspring of her life was broken. I greatly missed her warm affectionate nature, her sane sometimes humorous advice, and her moments of gaiety. Sometimes she had seemed more like a sister than a mother and my father had been a compelling influence over us both, in different ways. Now I felt that her going was the release of one who had lost all joy in life.

Like a ship that has cast off its mooring ropes, I felt there was nothing now to bind me to the old loyalties. I must, in a sense, set out again. There was something I still had to discover, and about which I must make a final decision.

At about this time we left the city and moved to a village a few miles outside it, partly for the health of the children. The atmosphere in this heavily industrial area was getting increasingly polluted, and our baby daughter was not thriving.

Here we bought a rambling Victorian house. To the children's joy it had two staircases, a pleasant enclosed garden, and even more enjoyable to them, a large cellar, where their small friends were put through strange initiation ceremonies. It was a solid homely house, which had seen one hundred years of life inside its thick stone walls. For almost the first time in our lives we felt we could settle, with some prospect of not moving again for a long time. We had been like 'displaced persons' so often, living in some sixteen different houses during the war, and then, since it ended, moving three times at brief intervals for the sake of Tom's work.

Now there was time to pause and to think, rather than to be rushed along by events. It was now we came to the final realisation that our minds were made up. For too long we had felt torn when the prospect of making a decision came before us; torn by the conflict between loyalty to those who had loved us and who had hoped to see us follow in their footsteps—for they were convinced that theirs was the right, the true way, based on 'sound' Biblical doctrine—and between loyalty to what we knew must be a far wider vision.

That first Sunday in the new house, Tom went with the little boys to a nearby parish Church, where he met and talked with the Vicar. We found later that he was a remarkable man in many ways. His unusual academic ability was coupled with a real power to inspire and to illuminate. He seemed a robust character, who had been in the Royal Navy; and with it all, he was warmhearted and natural. That morning he made Tom feel that he longed to help us, and to welcome us into the fellowship of this lively Church. It was a poor area between the mining belt and the country, and the Vicar was a man who lived simply, without any luxury or ostentation, caring only to carry the message of the Christian gospel to the neighbourhood. Many people, we found, travelled long distances to hear his inspirational preaching.

After several visits and discussions we felt we had found here a church where the Vicar, knowing our background, was glad to accept us just as we were. He was a man with a passion for evangelism in the good sense, and his views were broader than those to be found in some Anglican Churches. Before every service of Holy Communion, at which strangers were often to be found, he invariably issued the invitation to 'all those who love the Lord Jesus in sincerity, to all confirmed members of the Church of England'. To me, as a lay person, not at that time prepared to delve into deep theological issues, this seemed entirely right and in keeping with our Lord's teaching. My upbringing had left me with an inbred hatred of 'exclusivism' in any form. In fact there is much argument about this practice, many ordained men not feeling free to give such an open invitation. Others, even lecturers at certain Theological Colleges, hold that this practice had been traditional in the Church of England; and that while confirmation is entirely necessary for full membership of the Anglican Church, baptised members of other denominations should also be received at the service for occasional communion, if they so wish.

We talked with the Vicar quite often, enjoying the complete freedom of the discussion, the total lack of bigotry, and the atmosphere of friendliness. We began to realise that we could no longer remain uncommitted members of this community, standing on the fringe of the church, and in a way receiving without giving. We felt now that we must become confirmed members of the Church of England. We were ready for the final step. Yet 'final' is the wrong description. Rather, in Churchill's words, we knew we had to come to 'the end of the beginning'.

It was an end without any last scene of conflict, any dramatic breakaway. The struggle had taken place in the mind, over the years recorded in this book. Quite simply, it was over.

All that remained was to take our leave of those who had truly cared for us. Our friends among them accepted our motives, but their sadness was our only regret.

It was a chilly spring evening when Tom and I were confirmed with others both old and young. In that quiet moment men, women and young people made their public confirmation of the baptismal promise that they would 'endeavour' to 'keep God's holy will and commandments, and walk in the same all the days of their life'. I like the word 'endeavour'. It is an honest word. The way might be hard, and sometimes lonely, but the promise was not a rash one, for it was made in the light of its concluding words, 'God being my helper'.

Four friends who were travelling a similar path to ourselves came to be with us at this service. Subsequently one couple became members of the Church of England also; the others joined the Presbyterian Church. We had all received the strict grounding, the uncompromising teaching, and had all, I think, tried to retain what was good, but knew we must always claim freedom to do right as and when we saw it, and must never let any human being dictate our actions to us.

The elderly Bishop from overseas gave us practical advice for daily living. He was a saintly man whose words contained much shrewd wisdom, and I was impressed with the fact that although he was obviously a spiritual man, he was also in touch with everyday life.

The church to whose fellowship we now belonged stood strong and sturdy on a small hill; with its beautiful Norman tower facing the winds foursquare, it dominated the straggling pit village below, whose small dreary streets huddled on the hillside beside the working men's club, the small cluster of shops and the pubs. Behind the church stood a great slag heap, stark against the cold sky, in outline like a small mountain. Here we were in the heart of the tough world that had seen unemployment, poverty and hardship, whose men and women had long since learned to be suspicious of words without deeds, and promises without fulfilment. Below the hill the great river Tyne ran past, grey and often turbulent when the icy wind stormed up the broad valley. We were on the edge of the country, but here the church spoke primarily to the working man in an area of heavy industry.

It seemed right to be confirmed in such a place, where

much of our life was to be. The act itself seemed rather a strange step, at that moment of time. It was perhaps, for me, a step in a forward progression, almost like leaving a cloister, and setting out on a mountain track. The greatest freedom was to be oneself—with all one's failings and weaknesses. No one now demanded that we should subscribe to a rigid interpretation of certain doctrines and a strict code of behaviour patterns.

We were welcomed that evening into a world-wide family whose great strength lies in its diversity. Men of all shades of belief and all stages of progress have their home here; but all assent to the one creed which part by part becomes significant to them as they grow in faith and perception. I believe that because of its open attitude to all men, its acceptance of people just as they are, the Anglican Church has much to teach the stricter denominations. Our Lord's method was not, as I see it, initially to force men and women into a strict pattern or mould so that their freedom was limited, but it was so to affect them with the dynamic of his personality, so to pass on to them his spirit, that they found they had a new and 'abundant' life, which in its power and joy and hope could not fail to make them new creatures.

I soon found that in so far as the individual churches of this communion showed the true compassionate and redemptive love of Christ to its members and the world outside, they made an impact. In so far as they were not concerned for the outsider and the lonely, the sick and the starving, the wrongdoer and the unloveable man, they made no contact with the world.

'Inasmuch as ye did it not to one of the least of these ye did it not to me,' are burning words at the heart of the gospel which should never be forgotten.

How truly right is the Abbé Quoist in his book *Prayers of Life*, when he says: 'The Father has put us into the world, not to walk through it with lowered eyes, but to search for him through things, events, people.'

I suppose this book has been about a search; a search for freedom, and so, paradoxically, for God. It began, in a way, in a spirit of rebellion, at a sheltered, sometimes difficult, childhood. But human encounters, daily happenings, the very stuff of life itself, make the scene where the individual soul can turn to or from a faith. And so with me.

I have learnt to see over the years, so much more clearly, that much of my upbringing was good: the love, the security, without which a child dies. The strict disciplines, the loneliness, may have been a strengthening influence. My father's unswerving faith made me realise the potential power of true Christianity.

I recognise now that, in the words of George Patterson, missionary explorer-statesman in Tibet, that the Plymouth Brethren as I knew them, and he was one, were a people with 'a passion for God'. Their separation from the world was the result of their desire to walk with him. As I saw it, they were mistaken in this attitude. Some were even Pharisaical. They sometimes stifled natural emotions and joys, and forbade innocent pleasures, and this gave rise to other more insidious faults of intolerance and rigidity. And in so many ways they were 'apart'.

It is my belief that if Christianity is to have any reality, it must be lived out right in the world, in the centre of the arena. There, where life is toughest, right alongside the hopeless, the helpless and the wrongdoer, God is so often to be found. For 'he who has begun to give himself to others is saved. In receiving his neighbour he will receive God and will be freed from himself.'* This I believe, is for some, where the search ends and discovery begins. It was so with me.

Yet in spite of this, I saw in the Brethren, from time to time, true piety, quiet joy and simple sincerity. They were

* Michel Quoist, *Prayers of Life*.

inflexible and unyielding in holding to those beliefs which they felt were true and right. They were prepared to face great unpopularity with courage and calm. They asked no reward, and they held the world well lost, so that they might win Christ.

. . . . .

It would be idle to pretend that life has always been simple or easy since that Spring evening. Often it has not. It has sometimes been hard and demanding, sometimes lonely, but always worth while.

Over and above the difficulties, there is an endless sense of adventure—and fun. We are not a family who ever gets bored. We can laugh, not least at ourselves, and our children have an irrepressible sense of humour, a delight in the ridiculous, so that riotous comedy often intervenes to break tension and frustration.

Indeed life has been full of surprising and amusing situations unknown in my previous career. Within four years I had spoken to innumerable womens' meetings on a variety of subjects—I can only suppose it is hard to get anyone to perform these alarming tasks, and stunned at the honour of being asked, it never occurred to me to refuse—I had presided at two musical festivals, had opened two church bazaars, and one church garden party. For this last, a seemly feathered hat was purchased with some difficulty, to hide the quaking emotions, and to put 'a good face' on the whole situation, which was something of an ordeal. With beaming clerics at the elbow, I shouted into a little crackling microphone, which, with apparently malign intent, reproduced one's voice alternately in a fainting whisper and a parade ground roar. As I progressed from the stalls to the hoop-là, swept on to the putting green, had a crack at the coconut shy, imminent peril to the feathered hat, dived into the bran tub, ecclesiastical bodyguard ever at the ready to haul me out, and finally sank exhausted at the tea tables, the splendid bouquet now falling limp over one arm, I felt like some hybrid species that had dropped unexpectedly from another planet.

Surely it was not for this I had become a member of the Anglican Church! Of course it was not. This may have been a little evidence that at long last we 'belonged' somewhere. But the real purpose is gradually emerging over the years as something far deeper.

My husband has led a full and busy professional life, but his life in the Church has been even dearer to him. He was made one of the Vicar's Churchwardens after a time, and later a Lay Reader; and when eventually the Vicar moved to another Parish he gave Tom a beautiful prayer-book. In it he had written Tom's name, and after it he had inscribed the words, 'beloved friend, helper, and Churchwarden, Co-worker in the Gospel'. We were very moved.

Recently Tom spent four years studying and working in the evenings at the Bishop's class for mature laymen who hope ultimately to be ordained. Now the time for this draws near.

It has been quite surprising to find that in the eyes of some friends, I am an object of pity on this score. I do not think they understand that we welcome the challenge and the adventure, although I have no doubt at all it will bring many new problems.

To stagnate is to die; but for us, in this venture, there is a kind of excitement, as there must always be when a man is ready to do what he believes God wants of him.

As for me, the Church is the place to which I can turn for help and inspiration, and in the Sacrament for forgiveness and grace. But I have never changed my view that it is fully in the world that one should live. A personal faith can be an anchor in the storms of life, it can bring hope where there might well be despair, and I believe it is always strengthened by being a 'shared' faith within the community the Church affords. But to remain within the safe retreat seems contrary to the whole spirit of Christianity, whose Founder sent his followers 'out into all the world'. For here, where man is so often sad and lost, however much he may try to disguise this, not least from himself, the Christian qualities of compassion, humility and caring have never been more needed.

As I have written these pages I have sometimes seemed, in imagination, to hear the voice of Evangelist in *Pilgrim's Progress*, and the words ring out, firm and clear: 'Do you see yonder shining light?'

The answer of Christian, beginning his journey, as he gazes into the distance, is my answer, and that of many others: 'I think I do.' The voice speaks again, strong and sure: 'Keep that light in your eye, and go up directly thereto: so shalt thou see the gate . . .'

Then, it seems, I am watching a great company of pilgrims who have passed and are still passing through the centuries, whose differences are forgotten for they are united in one love, and together seek a country, and in this search they have found Life. Now the voice of Mr. Valiant-for-Truth speaks for them, and for all those who have loved and followed their Master, through doubts and difficulties, perils and hardship: 'My marks and my scars I carry with me to be a witness for me that I have fought his battles who now will be my Rewarder.'

. . . . .